THE WAY TO A *Greater Life*

The Way
to a
Greater Life

Glenda Green

Spiritis

ISBN: 978-0-692-36836-7

First edition, first printing January 2015

Spiritis Publishing

PO Box 21744
Aransas Pass, TX 78335

www.lovewithoutend.com

To my husband Dr. Larry Jensen,
Who walked the path with me; who always believed in me,
and whose love and wisdom
gave me strength through many years
of personal growth and transformation.

Table of Contents

Introduction

I cannot imagine anyone avoiding the pleasure and clarity of more light. Yet, I am continually surprised that so many in the silent majority prefer dark cloisters of conformity, which neither comfort nor lead to a better life. Ironically, we often feel safer in the shadows of under-exposure than we do in the light of clear and responsible joy.

Light is easy to find. It's everywhere. The secret to gaining and radiating more of it is having an unbiased connection with life. To the degree that our experiences are secondary, cloned from agreements or our own past perceptions and conclusions, our light is dimmed. Then, to the degree that veiled perceptions or wrongful beliefs have resulted in harm, damage, or failure, we are inclined to remain under the cover of darkness.

Light is most especially important to our spiritual awakening. People all over the world, in all religions, are turning away from orthodox practice, as they look for a more personal and direct experience of Divinity. This is almost inevitable with religious dogma losing some credibility against an expanding horizon of modern knowledge, research, and global interaction. Religious atrocities of the past can no longer be denied or justified, nor the fallibility of clergy who abused their positions of trust.

At the same time, we must also not forget that all of our great movements toward freedom were preceded by periods of enlightenment in which our faith in a higher Power (or at least consciousness) was regenerated. In most cases this elevation of consciousness came through our religious and spiritual convictions. It would be a dreadful mistake to forfeit the great treasures of our heritage. There is one inescapable fact to consider, which makes it easier to forgive mistakes and errors within our history: the more valuable something is to us, the more likely it will be exploited by villains and tyrants for their own dark ends. What causes our judgment and anxiety about recurring oppression is that its past appearance was in **in something we needed and valued. Thus our clear resolve about the future is inhibited.**

We are presented with choices and selectivity even in our sacred pathways. Jesus was tempted many times in his mission on earth. This is a frequent challenge for anyone in any age. However, at this time in history we have more from which to choose. It has never been more important that our choices be clearly presented. The mystical roots of Christianity, and the obscure people who kept it alive, are more relevant than ever to our contemporary search for spiritual direction and meaning.

I hope this book will show and honor how many people in the past faced similar options of conforming to dogma or electing a more direct approach to spiritual truth. Wisdom has always come with a price and with dedication to higher principles above just those of appearance, ritual, and doctrine. We are called, each one, to be discerning and responsible for our own awakening. In fact, a reliable standard by which to make all subjective decisions in life could be as simple is this. Which way will help me awaken? Which way will put me to sleep?

A few days ago I made a new acquaintance who asked me how I spent my time. I responded that I was writing a book about the mystical nature of Christianity. Her reply was, "Isn't that a contradiction in terms?" After a little bit of inquiry I found that she had been raised in a family steeped in religious protocol, limitations, and guilt. Her spiritual growth was stifled until later she found release and true inspiration in more loving beliefs. She was amazed to learn that Christianity had its roots in mysticism, and originally advocated direct experience with God.

In fact the earliest followers of Jesus referred to his teaching as "The Way." Although there were some initial disputes over non-Jews deviating from orthodox practices of food and hygiene, those arguments were soon lost in the explosion of new faith as it moved into many other cultures, adapting to local needs and practices as it spread. There was little need for doctrinal conformity until Christianity was sponsored and then controlled by Rome in the fourth century. However, the truth of its origins was never lost, and the heroic lives of its mystical converts are the most stirring and dramatic stories within its history. Many of them were beatified as saints.

In 1991 I joined the legions of men and women who have attained a direct experience of God through connection with Jesus Christ. It was a miraculous occurrence with extraordinary intent and consequences. What you are about to read is a progression of events leading toward his appearances to me, a short report of our conversations, and my personal evolution from visual artist to spiritual visionary, with all the challenges of bringing those realizations into a modern world with no easy model for doing so.

To that, I have added my own research on the subject of mysticism. Most especially, this book pays tribute to those who have lived and triumphed throughout history by demonstrating that such insight is not only natural to us; but, it may well be the leading edge of our consciousness, appearing in countless ways beyond defined religious practices.

Personally, I believe that Jesus was referring to our innate and profoundly spiritual capacity to receive direct revelations from God, when he said: "These things I do, you shall do and greater..." (John 14:12) In our wishful hearts we might prefer to believe he was referring to compassion in that statement. However, in my decades of observation about human nature, I have come to see that, while love is innate to our nature, compassion is not. Compassion comes only after much ego surrender, years of service to life and others, and dedication to the higher principles of humanity. This higher love, which the Greeks called Agape, is the fruit of our devotion to something greater than one's mortal self. The starting point is awakening consciousness, with its vast potential—wherein we acknowledge by faith what is beyond our current perception.

Human beings, throughout the ages and in all cultures, have demonstrated an expanse and fertility of consciousness that exceeds all other forms of life on earth. In this we have both an opportunity and a responsibility to connect all the dimensions of life as we know it. Many of those dimensions are best explored scientifically, while others can only be reached through instincts beyond all logic.

To some degree this book is a companion to my best-selling book, *"Love Without End, Jesus Speaks,"* which was released in 1998 and has since been published in fourteen languages and sold over a million copies. In fact, some chapters in this book were once included in the first edition of that one. Those parts were removed essentially because of personal content that was not yet fulfilled in my being. Yet, I hoped at some point those subjective experiences would become the seed of a much greater realization and offering to others. Perhaps this has now happened, and this book will stand on its own as testimony to the wealth of potential that comes from human awakening.

It is not necessary that you have read *"Love Without End,"* but if you have; and you wondered if there was more to the story, then this will answer many of your questions. If you have had a mystical experience yourself, whether an epiphany in life or a near-death experience, this book may provide many insights for how to share those experiences with others. Most of all, if you have dreamed of how far you can pursue your own spiritual vision, and still live a lucid and socially relevant life, perhaps this will give you a model that is almost unavailable in contemporary literature, even with all the research into consciousness and spirituality.

In his beautiful little work, *"The Lost Dimension,"* Hugh I'Anson Fausset wrote: "To be human is to bring the

Kingdom of Light down to earth and to raise up earth to heaven."

This inspires us to think that perhaps the link we seek to a better life is actually within our own nature and being. As an artist, teacher, writer, and counselor, I have had marvelous glimpses of scalable reality that stretches further than I ever thought possible. My wish is this book will help you discover the greater portion of all that you are, as well as your own place in the link between heaven and earth.

Glenda Green M.A., D.D., 2015

Chapter 1

Our Miraculous Universe

There is light our eyes cannot see. Yet, we follow by faith. When we are awestruck by the heavens at night, wonder what calls the butterflies into migration, or think about the amazing power of love we are touched by a greater light, which seamlessly weaves all the threads of our miraculous universe. At such moments we are called away from our smallness and allowed to glimpse, if only for an instant, at the splendor of infinity.

Then, in a flash we lose the vision; not because the universe is jealous of what we have seen, but because we refocus on our world as a practical context in which to live. And, so it is, the universe graciously reduces its scale so that we may find comfort in what it provides for our immediate interests and needs.

Our universe is sublimely adaptable and coherent, yet its uncharted terrain is so great as to baffle our logical mind. No doubt, if all were known, we would think it quite simple. However, considering the richness and complexity of our experience, I somehow think we will never decrease our sense of awe in the face of infinity. It is not by coincidence that we humans exist somewhere in the middle between giant Quasars and subatomic particles. This is not happenstance because the perspective in both directions is from our own center of being!

How much of existence is united because we see it that way? How much appears to be unreal or chaotic because it exceeds the grasp of our understanding? How facile and creative is our consciousness in uniting the many venues for explaining reality? Will we try to explain the unknown with logic, or will we use creative imagery to summon a new belief?

Mankind lives an eternal paradox. We have been given the blessing of knowing that "we are", and also the challenge of knowing we are "part of" something much greater than our self. Our abilities, interests, and affections all contribute to our personal character, and yet we were given to know a larger 'Self' found only through connections to one another and with nature. We are often stumped with how to explain our relationship to the universe. We have explored it, researched it, written about it, speculated and dreamed about it, and often received answers of both a scientific and spiritual nature. Still, we do not understand.

In my mystical journey I have encountered other subtle qualities we normally do not see, which can be found in the dawn and the twilight moments of changing reality where a doorway opens that we may enter. Or, perhaps we will pass and pretend it was not there. Only in such fleeting glimpses are we able to see the whole of our own being in silhouette against the grandeur of the universe. What treasures we have in the works of such great artists as Van Gogh who opened his soul to vast perceptions. Despite the starkness and poverty of his physical life, he stood in a field alone. Inside his own vastness he commemorated that moment of union with a grand "Starry Night."

Regardless of the path we choose, or the reality we embrace, the amazing part of it all is how life coordinates, integrates, and synthesizes all of its parts into seamless harmony, even within our self. Coherence, it seems, is the very goal of creation and consciousness. The universe does not require of us, or even offer to us, an understanding of all its secrets. That is our curiosity alone and a challenge for our growth. What it requires of us is an endless search and respect for unity in all of life as we expand our awareness through symbiotic response. In many ways, coherence is the primal force of what we call love. From another perspective it is the fiber and strength of conscious evolution and personal responsibility.

To redeem any part of our life we only need to consider the greater whole to which we belong, and open ourselves to a grander perspective. Through an elevation of consciousness we are more able to unify and transcend the scattered parts of any challenged reality. Wholeness and healing have much in common. However, in our bodies, minds, and souls, wholeness is not the result of healing. Healing is the result of wholeness pursued with dedicated effort and desire. The power of wholeness is so intense, so unflinching, that it will draw from every level of potential, revealing possibilities we would not have thought possible. What we see, in essence, is a miracle.

The most common reluctance I find in some people to pursue a more spiritual life is the fear of "falling to pieces" or "dropping off the deep end." This is amusing and ironic, to say the least, considering that a person deficient in spiritual consciousness is already "living in pieces."

As we seek to know, and open ourselves to the vast "Unexpected," our lives actually come together. We look for that great, invisible, intangible inner force that knits all parts of our self and the world into some manner of accord. Even though many sectors of our life are far from perfect, we could not be a whole person if we did not already have within us the same force that binds and directs the universe into a symphonic masterpiece. Even when reactive thoughts or actions influence us, there is still a larger force that allows us to develop and hold some redeeming resolution.

The power that draws life together (which can be summarized as love) is so vital to our being that we incrementally damage ourselves to the degree that we deny it, harm it, or misdirect it. That insurmountable drive can place before us new possibilities, unseen by our ordinary senses, and yet sensed by some sinews of coherence within us. The fact that any one of us is whole in a universe bursting with random energy, on a planet with endless adaptations of bacteria competing for protein—that our body and being were ever assembled and remained protected—is a miracle.

Perhaps the greatest miracle of all is that we are here and consciously aware, not only of the universe, but ourselves. How much love was required for that to happen? We are both the result and the cause of that which is joined together in a continuously creative and created flux. That is cause for wonder!

Wise teachers through the ages have said that by faith, and whatever measure of consciousness we possess, all the dimensions of our reality can partake of a higher nature. There is also a higher sense of reason in this, which is more spherical and expanding than linear. When one understands the implications of a truly unified field, valid under all conditions, then practical, scientific, and sublime realities are all connected.

Unity can be attained, and one of the greatest mysteries of the universe can be solved: namely, our relationship to the Creator and our causal participation in the evolution of consciousness. This realization must happen personally through direct experience; and, our universe is designed exactly to allow that fulfillment. Such an attainment is not in any way an intellectual accomplishment. It is not reserved for those in privileged positions or available only to the learned. Often it happens to the most innocent and unprepared, but it is nonetheless an advanced encounter with Consciousness.

Pursuit of conscious evolution is innate and natural to human beings when not interfered with by tyranny and oppression; conditions which directly result in ignorance. Let there be no mistake, ignorance is as cultivated as higher education. It does not exist in the innocent, even though limitations of learning and experience may be present. Therefore, let us begin by looking at our natural tendencies for explaining life. One of the most natural inclinations is to look for connections between cause and effect. Babies do this; animals exhibit this natural tendency; and, just as surely, plants turn their leaves toward the sun.

We seek the predictable, and at the same time we hope for the most positive response from forces outside our self. This is what Jesus was encouraging us to believe when he referred to lilies of the field and how they toiled not but wore the raiment of kings. (Matthew 6:28)

We plan for our needs with rational expectations of cause and effect, but we also dream of exceptional possibilities that break the mold of ordinary patterned experience. We all know this can happen. Somewhere in between these two extremes we look for probabilities that might allow us to move our reasonable and manageable life a little closer to the threshold of our dreams. Instinctively we are drawn to the most rewarding perspective of all: that of unity, the basis for sustainable connection between all manifestations of reality

Orderly structure and exceptional possibility are not mutually repellant. To the contrary, none of us could exist for long without both. They are alternating forms of opportunity, one for predictable continuity, the other for change. Because all order is subject to change, unexpected opportunities can appear under any set of conditions. Thus, we are released from the tyranny of outmoded structures and presented with new opportunities to realize our highest aspirations. Anything can be reshaped through inserting a new thought, intention, feeling, impulse, or action. Each participant in life can and will generate new possibilities and ignite an unplanned expansion of reality. We all possess this power, and through being open to a greater consciousness we can directly contribute to a greater way of living.

Even though some people are reluctant to admit that miracles happen, it is amazing how much we all live our daily lives fully counting on them. If you consider how many variables and risks are involved in driving twenty miles on a four-lane freeway, it is a sheer miracle to arrive home safely. We only have to look at life with innocent perception to see how much miracles are part of daily experience.

The fact is, life holds together despite its frequent rearrangements. Through expansions that exceed our imagination, and through setbacks, disasters, and oppressions that exceed our tolerance, life still holds together. Sometimes unity can be maintained only by extraordinary compensation from powers normally unseen. There is a force of coherence that offers potential for unity and meaning in every situation even if we do not always realize it.

In seeing a miracle, the greatest obstacle anyone will encounter both within oneself and among others is that of judgment and restrictive beliefs. All of our limitations in life are rooted in limited perspectives about what is possible. When I say 'limited' I am referring to a fixed point of view that remains essentially the same regardless of how much new experience and data may be available to it.

It is largely because of fixed ideas that we fend off the miraculous potential within reality and we recoil in skepticism toward those who do see it. We are not prepared to accept that many of the structures in which we have placed our faith are simply illusions of order and not profound organization. It's quite a shock when predictable order is completely dismantled—even if it's with the most benevolent result! I sometimes think we would prefer to suffer oppression than to have our desires fulfilled in an unpredictable way. When confronted with the fragile illusion of what we thought was real, we are shaken to our core.

Fortunately, we are at a point in history where our spiritual luminaries and our greatest scientists concur on one important point: that is all of existence is connected in a unified and expanding system and that it has an amazingly resilient and creative way of maintaining its coherence.

It is only our sleeping consciousness, and the way we give away our few waking moments to feed some pre-existing beliefs. This prevents a larger vision of life from creating new perspectives. Once upon a time, we thought the earth was flat; and then we expanded our belief to hold that physical reality could be explained fully by a three-dimensional model of mass, energy, and space. In the twentieth century Albert Einstein added the fourth dimension of time, yet he did so with caution that we not expect it to mark the outer limits of what was possible. We have now gone so far beyond that edge as to be concerned with how to explain and connect multi-dimensions of existence, and layers of universes. Yet, "coherence" is still the operative word. That is one of the basic drives of both existence and consciousness; but, how it will reduce to mechanics and mathematics in the new paradigm is yet to be seen.

For the moment, what this larger vision offers to the evolution of our consciousness and to our spiritual understanding is immense. Scientists, philosophers, and a new generation of mystics are modeling a revolutionary view of the universe as expanding spherically and infinitely, potentially unified **from any point within the whole.**

The ancient Greek philosophers saw the need for expanding their explanations of life, but they could only develop thought in two directions. They considered how creation began, and then explained how subsequent progressions resulted from it. Logic is a system of thinking used to explain cause and effect. This is the language of science and reason.

They also considered the unique and special power of Divine Origin, which they called Logos. The word Logos has often been used in reference to the original generative Force…the Source of All…The Truth! For the Greek philosophers, Logos was the prime postulated truth that provided an explanation for beginnings, and also provides a "constant," or framework, in which logic unfolds, as well as the character of what has been created.

According to the Greeks, one of the most remarkable attributes of Logos is the way it guides our actions through both faith and logic, often without revealing itself or the true nature of our actions until we are well into the creative process. Then somewhere in the middle of its evolution, comes the great 'ah ha'! At that point the greater reason appears, the pieces fall into place, and the holistic nature of what we are doing takes over. I sometimes think what we call a miracle is just the visible emergence of Logos (the greater reason) which was there all along, but which we could not see until some unexpected window presented an expanded view. This is as true as it ever was.

Classical logic continues to be true and relevant wherever linear progressions and comparative extremes matter. For example, we can measure white more accurately against a backdrop of black; and, any perception of one extreme carries with it a subtle reminder of the other. As an extension of logic there are progressions (time) and boundaries (space). Logic is basically the study of what comes from what, and in what context. It's the study of progressions and derivatives: how something came to be what it is. At the level of derivatives, all of life is just an effect becoming another effect. In this complex network of associated meanings, we use comparisons to sort out the confusion and make sense of life. In a moral context, we use explanations of good and evil to discern constructive and destructive possibilities.

However, logic cannot circumscribe the holistic nature of life. Logic also cannot explain or embrace the origins of the universe, or a human soul, or even an idea. As a matter of fact, it cannot explain origins at all. Beginnings, by definition, are not derivative. The nature of beginnings can range from presumed states of absolute origin to spontaneous or serendipitous mutations within some kind of pre-existent context. It was to this end that the Greeks proposed and pondered the power of Logos. In their world view they found reconciliation between Logos and logic. Today, there is even greater evidence that Logos and logic are fully reconcilable into a new, more comprehensive, explanation.

However, Western culture did inherit a deep prejudice against any exploration of consciousness that could not be accountable to theology, science, or visibly reveal some order of progression. Other dimensions of awareness, and sudden eruptions of spontaneous potential, were always regarded suspiciously. In Greece, Rome, and all their descendant cultures, there was no place for consciousness that could not be controlled and adjusted either to fit logic or the moral values determined by theocratic leaders. That is the main reason we do not associate mysticism with Western thought, yet find it so richly part of every other culture. For centuries, Western Culture would be affected by a predominant focus on the material world, one that regards the Divine as an unapproachable source of perfection unknowable to ordinary humans.

Albert Einstein was confronted with the limited framework of classical philosophy as he studied the nature of light. He quickly realized the limits of Newtonian physics as well. He postulated that light was a dynamic constant for all time and space. In order to demonstrate this, he first had to present a new idea of infinity-based logic, which we now call relativity. The universe was no longer viewed through a scale of comparative extensions, but from a constant observable in all things. Interestingly, light behaves both as a linear wave form and also as a spontaneous particle, thus applying to all forms of behavior. The holistic result is our understanding of a universe fully integrated and similar from particle systems to cosmic systems.

With such lack of intellectual support for mysticism in Western culture many students of early Christianity, especially referring to Gnostic ideas, just assumed those strangely exotic beliefs migrated from Asian culture, and lost their fire as Christianity was Romanized. What they missed is that Jesus was himself, a true mystic, regardless of where he may have traveled or studied. His teachings were not about religion (certainly not an orthodox one) so much as direct communion with God and "the way" to a greater light.

Mystical perceptions are often the harbinger of rapid evolutions of consciousness that have no pre-existing model for justification. Perceptions and experiences have transcended conventional and limiting ideas about how things are supposed to be. Consciousness takes care of the revelation; we simply have to respond.

One of the most fascinating attributes of consciousness is the way it correlates our inner and outer reality, revealing these connections **only as they are lived.** This is the mystical "extra measure" of life—the one that cannot be predicted or explained by dogmatic beliefs of any kind, theological or scientific.

Ironically, our best explanation of this phenomenon has been advanced by David Bohm, the renowned quantum physicist. In his theory of "implicate and explicate order" he has actually proposed a new cosmology that views universal order in a radically different way from anything that has come before. Ordinary forms, including time, space, and energy, even abstractions about them, he considers to be the explicate manifestations of enfolded (implicate) order of everything that ever could exist.

Bohm and other scientists of the last thirty years have created landmarks of liberty for how we think about life. Even though their objectives have been scientific, they have given a wider berth to consciousness, which cannot be bridled by limiting agreements. Their theories provide the most likely answers so far as to why our human consciousness reaches the limit of any linear direction and must reconnect with a larger whole in order to continue its growth.

In Bohm's conception of order, the undivided whole and the implicate order inherent within it, is primary rather than particles, quantum states, or even time and space. For Bohm, 'The Whole' encompasses all things, structures, abstractions and processes, including processes that resolve into stable structures as well as those that result in metamorphosis. His description of this idea is amazingly spiritual and poetic: "The new form of insight can perhaps best be called Undivided Wholeness in Flowing Movement. This view implies that flow is, in some sense, prior to that of the 'things' that can be seen to form and dissolve in this flow." Thus, according to Bohm's view, the whole is in continuous flux, and hence is referred to as the holo-movement—movement of the whole.

This is what mystics have reported since time immemorial. They were moved by life into their greater realizations about it. Their revelations sprung from a deeper order that has its own patterns, ways, and timing. Such moments of heightened consciousness, where our smaller world ends and the greater one begins, cannot be estimated through linear time and space nor constrained by theological dogma. As individuals we are very small; and yet we partake of a vast potential that defies our definition of it.

Knowing this brings liberty. It allows for the expression of free will and for integrating various realities in a positive and tolerant way. There is an enduring state of dynamic equilibrium that sustains the patterns of cause and effect and yet allows for unpredictable and transcendent events. Within it all there is the power of Consciousness, expanding always beyond any lesser forces that would attempt to restrict it. If we would behold a miracle, we must first behold the miracle of reality—that its unity is seamless—that it can provide a different experience for each of us, and yet be consistent for all. This is indeed an amazing universe. When we shift from linear predictability to spherical and expanding unity we find whole new possibilities. From this perspective all manner of new realizations are possible and we are set free to explore life without having to know what is around every bend of the road. We will discover our destiny **as we live it.**

Chapter 2

Precognitions

In the best of all possible worlds it seems we would find our way easily on whatever journey we embarked. And yet, in the best of all possible worlds we would wish intensely for so many possibilities as to never tire from exploration. Perhaps God has answered both prayers by giving us a universe that is reliably practical, infinitely open to miracles, and yet mysterious enough to challenge our conscious evolution. Through countless dimensions of reality and possibility, the dialog between heaven and earth never ends. We see it in the eternal connection between thought and manifest reality; and, in the inspirations and visions that impel extraordinary quests. We see it in the playful dance of predictability and surprise. Stretching from science and philosophy to the dreams of our heart, we seek to discover the quivering gossamer edge of existence where there is no lesser realm.

Within the infinite stream of time, there are points where our stories begin to take shape. But, rarely are they all revealed at once. The greater forces that shape our lives are quite clever in the way they dart through the trees and wrap their golden threads around a forest too large and dense for us to see beyond. Perhaps these forces need to gestate in the womb of life until the right convergence of factors brings them to light. Perhaps they are so deeply rooted in our own nature we have no objectivity on them. One thing is for certain: they are much easier to see in hindsight.

By a strange set of ironies, in the fall of 1967 I found myself at Tulane University beginning study for a Master's Degree in art history. My hope and original postulate was to pursue a Master of Fine Art degree in painting, at the University of Indiana, or Columbia University, both of which had accepted my applications. However, destiny was unfolding in other directions. My application for scholarships, which were essential for continued study, were lost or delayed by factors outside my control. Instead, a wild card application to study art history at Tulane's Newcomb College was not only accepted but had been awarded one of the largest fellowship grants in the United States.

There was always next year to try again for painting, and rather than waste the gift, I decided that it would not hurt my professional range to have a full historical understanding of art to complement my creative intentions. I had visions of studying the great Renaissance masters, or the beautiful richness of Impressionism, all of which would only expand my appreciation and technical understanding for my own later creations. What was there to lose?

I believed this would be a pleasant diversion, with minimum challenge, or so I thought. It was also in New Orleans. What a place to spend a couple of years. However, by a turn of events I could not have anticipated, my free will in all of this was intercepted once again. One of the stipulations for the Kress Fellowship was that I studied with the senior professor of the faculty, who just happened to be a specialist in Early Christian and Medieval art history. She was a brilliant person who had joined the Tulane faculty from a high standing rank at the University of Cologne. Most definitely, it was an honor to study with her, but how would this satisfy the creative stimulus for paintings I would later resume? On meeting her, I was impressed by her impeccable mind and charmed by her delightful German accent, although it was hard to follow her lectures, and her bibliography for study was mostly in European languages, with some even in ancient languages.

What had I gotten myself into? I thought I was doomed for wash-out before mid-terms, and then an extraordinary thing happened. I surrendered to the idea of doing my best even if defeat was inevitable. I decided to invest my ample stipend toward hiring other students to translate for me. German, French, Italian, Spanish, and Latin: That was just the beginning of what was to come. I revised my personal schedule so that I was up all night, and my early morning classes would come at the end of my work day when I was at my primed best. Then I would sleep. For a semester at least, I could forfeit daylight for a greater purpose. My dedication was total, and I completely forgot my own reservations and resistance to this new twist of fate. Even though I would not have chosen this course of study, it was so different and so challenging as to unlock doors of curiosity way beyond the veneer of casual fascination. Somehow I was plummeted into depths (or perhaps heights) of consciousness that were far beyond the structure of logical thinking. Pretty soon I was dreaming of these ancient times and speaking their languages in my dreams. Not more than six weeks passed before I was joining my translators in reading directly from the texts once completely foreign to me. Then I was on my own, reading adequately, if not proficiently, all the texts that thwarted me in the beginning.

After my first term paper was graded, Dr. Davis (my professor) added a special note that she was so glad to have a student who was this well prepared linguistically. Little did she know it had taken me four years of college Spanish, using traditional methods of study, just to speak a few words of that language.

What I could not tell anyone, because I did not understand it myself at the time, is I had stumbled on a deeply seated "Rosetta Stone" of linguistic consciousness that probably exists in all of us when we are born. This faculty may be why children are so fluid with language and can learn any language to which they are born.

The only way I can explain my personal recovery of that ability is that my depth of dedication had immersed me into some extra potential available for its consummation. Or was there a factor of destiny that overrode my normal limitations?

This later possibility began to suggest itself after the success of my first semester, when Dr. Davis summoned me to her office to hear a new proposal. It was time to decide on a research direction for my master's thesis, and she had a special topic she had been reserving until the right student came along. With my "excellence for language," she felt it would be a natural next step to begin reading in ancient languages, which were required for the topic she was about to present. I cannot begin to tell you how many bees were swarming in my head as I collapsed into a quiet panic in the chair opposite her desk.

A native of Germany, she had the privilege of studying the great medieval cathedrals of Germany and France first hand, touching the cool stone and having lunch in the shadows of their beauty. She was also fascinated with the parallel emergence of a people's reality that showed up in the plays enacted on the porches of the great cathedrals. In earlier times, these were morality plays or enactments directly from the Bible. But as centuries rolled by, and a people's culture and language also evolved, these stories became encased in contemporary reality and romance epics. For example, the story we know today as Cinderella, was originally a parable of the beleaguered church often oppressed and put into servitude by the dark sisters of feudal wealth and power. Prince Charming was the Christ who would awaken the church's heart and restore its true place in the palace of heaven. Parallels of meaning, such as this were hidden in most, if not all, of medieval theater. And most, if not all, theater was played on the great Cathedral porches. That way, as audiences were enthralled with Tristan and Isolde, the background on the tympanum (arch over the doorway) would be resplendent with carved stories from the Bible to inspire thoughts on that level.

The Morality Plays (as they were called) had a potent effect on the evolution of style on French and German cathedrals, or perhaps it was a revelation of converging forces of culture and emerging popular vigor. Either way, theatrical costumes began to sway the dress in which sculpted religious figures were portrayed on the doorways. For over a thousand years of Christian art, Mary, Jesus, and all the saints had been portrayed only in Semitic dress or Roman tunics and togas (depending on the preference of those commissioning the sculpture). Then, suddenly, around 1180 on the porch of Reims Cathedral a figure of Joseph appears dressed in the fashionable attire of a common Frenchman!

Every nuance of style on this or any cathedral was rigidly controlled by theologians. So, what had changed? Nothing that was obvious. Nothing recorded in history books. Nevertheless, as Dr. Davis drank in the mysteries of this edifice, during her own study at the Sorbonne, she dared to ask some very provocative questions. As a student of medieval literature also, she had asked the same questions. The languages of emerging cultures, created by both indigenous and migrating people, contained legends, wisdom, and beliefs that went far beyond the structured and enforced limitations of official theology.

To be sure, extra measures of creativity can always be found in the flow of prevailing culture, in any epoch. Eventually, widespread common practices and beliefs will influence more privileged conformity. Dr. Davis's more important speculation was that the rising culture of Medieval France held within it the secrets of **hidden**

theology that could no longer be suppressed, because those secrets were known and practiced by so many people whose loyalty the church was cultivating. The people's culture, though considered vulgar by the church, would have provided the perfect cover and conveyance for mysteries the Church wanted to suppress. A populace illiterate of the written word found their own language of inspiration through theater and art. The perfect counter strategy of conservative theologians could have been to use the same popular ideals and images, and then direct them to their own end. From two directions, for complementary reasons, there were sudden eruptions of popular images in art, theater, and literature of the late Middle Ages.

This was a fascinating idea, but only special research could turn up evidence for its validity. That task she had saved for some future student who seemed ripe for the task. It would involve translating forty-two epic romance plays that had never been studied outside their original milieu. It would involve an in depth study of the lives and writings of medieval saints of the twelfth and thirteenth centuries who practiced a mystical life outside traditional theology, and in some cases were martyred for doing so. It would involve connecting this evidence to writings of the early church fathers, such as Origin and Augustine, who had alluded to different threads of practice within the faith, and to those who had formally dismissed the idea of a direct connection with God separate from the Church as an intercessor. It would also involve historical research about communities in medieval France that had been brutally persecuted for practicing mystical Christianity. And finally, it would involve a summation about how the rise of popular culture in the European late Middle Ages was the only vessel large enough to carry such a resurgent power of this ancient knowledge.

As if that were not daunting enough, Dr. Davis presented me with the idea that the Italian Renaissance, primarily financed by the Medici family and the Church, was a kind of counter-renaissance to the **real Renaissance** that happened in and around Paris a century earlier—that being a people's movement and not the 15th century intellectual movement, which came about in Italy. The fact is, Italy was pitiable in the century prior to **its** Renaissance: poor in wealth, health, morale, and industry, with many warring city-states. The only power it had was the Vatican and a few families that had become influential throughout Europe because of trade and banking during the later Crusades. By contrast, Paris was wealthy in everything from trade and industry to innovation, banking, and the arts, not to mention rich in its typical pride. There is no question that it was the most fertile ground for the birth of a free culture, and moreover, the populace was rich with enthusiasm to create it.

That day in her office I sat in rapt amazement at what had been dished onto my plate. What a privilege to hear her ideas. But, why me? I was overwhelmed with the magnitude of research this project implied, not to mention further linguistic miracles that would be necessary. One of my fellow classmates had just graduated with a thesis on Whistler's Mother. For heaven's sake, why couldn't I just write a summation of all the "Boating Parties" that Monet ever painted?

She made it clear that I did not have to make a decision that day, but somehow I knew I did have to respond quickly before my mind could assemble its resistance. As if in sudden death, all the months flashed through my memory of how I had come to this point because of other forces choosing for me. Then in an equally sudden flash of confidence, I sat up in my chair and quietly poised myself to say, "I'll do it." In that instant I realized that one true choice made in full deliberate consciousness, eradicates all the past choosing life has made for us. We do not have to choose everything. We just have to know that we **can choose**, and in crucial times when it really matters, to call forth that power.

Mundane as it may seem, this was the beginning of my direct experience of God through the power of my own choosing. Only then would I be ready to study with the great teachers I would find on the pages of history.

Chapter 3

Those Who Prepared the Way...

What I discovered on the pages of history, and within the hidden symbols of art and literature would change my life forever. There are many ways we are blessed by inspirations from higher realms, and most of them are dismissed today with arrogant assumptions that all truth is reducible to factual reports and logic. In the late Middle Ages this was not the case. There was vitality of spirit, which had not yet surrendered to any restrictive bridle. Their world gives witness to spiritual heroism not often seen in modern times. Innocence, virtue, and stunning imagination are boldly displayed against a field of dark medieval control, superstition, prejudice, and brutal injustice.

Within that starkly contrasting reality I found the key I was looking for: the catalytic forces, which can ignite change in any age. These forces are not externally applied to alter human predicaments, as with economic or political manipulation, but are indigenous to what makes us human. When crushed by stagnant conditions, which endanger our life or smother creation, a greater power will rise up within us to explore or create alternate directions. That power is nothing less than the very Consciousness which unites our common survival directing it into an evolutionary mandate. At its highest level, in all ages, expansion of consciousness activates our spiritual nature and reminds us that we are both body and soul—that we walk on the earth yet reach for the stars. Within that cauldron of possibilities, anyone who truly sought for higher truth could find personal experience of the Divine. This, in its purest form is mysticism. The resurgence of mysticism between 1100 and 1500 in Europe provided landmark evidence of its splendid power to generate a new age. Nothing so radical had happened since the first three hundred years of Christianity.

Mysticism is both familiar and unfamiliar within the traditions of Christian thought. If we feel a deep comfort within our soul, and a sense of leaping for the light, when we are offered the fruits of mystical life, it is because the beginning of what we call Christianity happened within the transcendent life and consciousness of Jeshua ben Joseph, the one we call Jesus Christ, whose truth caused the seed of our being to remember its Divine origin. I'm not sure he would recognize all that has happened in his name since he walked the streets of Jerusalem. Christianity has often been driven by the pursuit of political power and enforced by the most rigid doctrine. Yet in its darkest moments, the mystics—those who sought direct union with God—were holding the light. At times these two rivers of power (the mystical and the orthodox) formed a benevolent blend as they did in the first centuries after Jeshua's life. At other times any truth resulting in a schism was brutally suppressed by those who welded the sword of orthodoxy.

The period between AD 400 and 1400, is rightly named the dark ages. Those who held the light did so mostly sub-rosa. The fact that early Christians worshiped in secret did not really end at the legalization of Christianity in 425AD. It continued all through the middle ages and well into the modern era. The hiding places simply changed, and those they hid from wore different garments. Most of those who lived and died anonymously for their faith have remained so, although their legacy is one of immeasurable importance to our modern consciousness.

The purpose of this book is not so much to study the elements or practices of mysticism as it is to examine the mystical dimensions of our human psyche and our need to explore levels of consciousness beyond the ordinary. While mysticism has been a vital part of every culture, and can be found to varying degrees within every religion, the late Middle Ages in Europe offers a potent laboratory for studying the essential connection between mysticism and the evolution of human consciousness.

Contrary to the modern idea that consciousness only grows in the sterile conditions of scientific control, there is much evidence that consciousness cannot grow without equal progressions of personal insight and responsibility. And, that cannot happen without extraordinary perceptions of how one's life can make a difference in the natural order of shared existence. In no other period of history were guardians of power more mistrustful of the common man's aspiration to higher knowledge as they were in the late middle ages. After a thousand years of oppression, the human spirit was never more willing to make the ultimate sacrifice to reach for something better than a distant promise of heavenly benison as their reward. These seeds of change began to sprout in the lives of saints and geniuses, and also in the voice of extremists and radical movements, in songs, poems, plays, and the optimistic enterprises of a birthing middle class.

No doubt it was divine providence that led me to study this period of art, literature, and history. By personal inclination I would have shunned the very nature of life in this period, so stripped of luxury for the common man, so full of hardship, epidemics, bitter cold winters, and many cycles of famine, which held little potential for the creation of fine art—the very subject I had intended to study. However, God has a way of taking us one step (or many) further than we anticipate. Our own estimation of what we need to discover or experience usually falls short. What I was about to see through the lives of ancient poets, sculptors, play writes, and beloved saints was something far greater than the creation of art. It was the creation of a new world, and I was given an opportunity to witness the very elements present at its conception.

The Roman Catholic Church had been the single, largest unifying structure in medieval Europe. It touched everyone's life, no matter what their rank or class or where they lived. With the exception of a small number of Jews, everyone in Europe was a Christian during the middle ages from the richest king down to the lowest serf.

From the moment of its baptism a few days after birth, a child entered into a life of service to God and God's

Church. As a child grew, it would be taught basic prayers, would go to church every week barring illness, and would learn of its responsibilities to the Church. Every person was required to live by the Church's laws and to pay heavy taxes to support the Church. In return for this, they were shown the way to everlasting life and happiness after lives that were often short and hard.

In addition to collecting taxes, the Church also accepted gifts of all kinds from individuals who sought special favors or wanted to be certain of a place in heaven. These gifts included land, flocks, crops, and even serfs. Through its vast holdings the church became politically powerful as well as the vessel of Christ's messages into the world. In many cases it was more influential than kings over their own kingdoms.

As a way of life this could not endure against the ground-swell of a modern era emerging. Theological rigidity, not to mention political alliances and privately held economy were too vested and inflexible to mid-wife the birth of a new world. It was inevitable that the coming evolution would occur through popular movements, and many extreme doctrines which disavowed Catholic supremacy. It came through both bloodshed and ecstasy.

Chaos is the mother of change, good and bad, and by the twelfth century, Europe was ripe with both chaos and positive potential. My research began to reveal the presence of a deeper constant. Beneath the formidable towers of orthodoxy and feudal control, there was a quiet underground river evidenced only by the clear trickles of fresh water that some would catch in their cup of consciousness. That was an unshakable belief that human beings could and were responsible for their own lives. That we could and do have a direct personal connection with the Divine. This was the dawning of belief in personal sovereignty as confirmed by real experience of union with God. Once tasted, this restorative elixir would not remain in the bottle. Whether expressed in philosophical terms or through the inspiration of art, poetry, music, or ideals of personal liberty, it was a driving force of conviction which brought great courage.

The rise of national power, capitalism, banking, and the first scientific rumblings were much easier for the Church to assimilate and manipulate than the mystical convictions that were being spoken of in hushed voices and secret symbols. Nothing compared to the threat these mystical convictions posed to the Church, for those beliefs challenged the core of its power, namely that it could decide who would see heaven and why. To claim any other route to God was heresy.

Indeed, it was very dangerous to take any sort of stand against the Catholic Church, visible or otherwise. Nevertheless, by the twelfth century, the movement toward personal freedom was so large it could not be hidden. It was a major force with which to contend, and in one instance the Church initiated a huge and bloody war against the Languedoc region of what is now southern France. It was a 20-year military campaign waged only for the suppression of free thought. This Crusade also was instrumental in the creation and institutionalization of the extremely political Dominican Order and the Inquisition they conducted.

A Crusade as violent as any fought in the Middle East, it was called the Albigensian Crusade because of the large numbers of independent religious sects in and around the city of Albi, where, in 1176, a Church Council first declared their practices heretical.

The Roman Catholic Church had always dealt vigorously with strands of Christianity it considered heretical, but before the 12th century such groups were organized in smaller numbers. In the 12th century much of what is now Southern France was converting to threatening deviations from orthodoxy.

In 1209 some thirty thousand knights and foot soldiers from northern Europe descending like a whirlwind on the Languedoc -- the mountainous northeastern foothills of the Pyrenees. This deliberate extermination lasted for over twenty years and resulted in the death of an estimated 200,000 to 1,000,000 people.

The extermination of populations, cities, and crops was so extensive as to be called the first "genocide" in modern European history. In one town, for example, fifteen thousand men, women, and children were slaughtered wholesale—many of them in the sanctuary of the church. When an officer inquired of the Pope's representative how he might distinguish heretics from true believers, the reply was, "Kill them all. God will recognize his own."

Having been called by the Pope himself, its participants wore a cross on their tunics, like crusaders in Palestine, and their rewards were dispensations from the Church, such as remission of all sins, an suspension of penances, an assured place in heaven, and all the booty one could plunder. There has also never been a greater land seize on behalf of France.

What did the people of the Languedoc do to deserve such a crusade? Residents of the Languedoc practiced a civilized, easy-going religious tolerance, much like Byzantium. In contrast to the fanatical zeal that characterized other parts of Europe, the Languedoc was a place where learning and philosophy flourished, poetry and courtly love were extolled, and Greek, Arabic and Hebrew were enthusiastically studied. Schools devoted to the Kabala, the ancient exoteric tradition of Judaism, thrived. These people seemed to have adhered to a life of extreme devotion and simplicity. Deploring churches, they usually conducted their rituals and services in the open air or in any readily available building—a barn, a house, a municipal hall. They also practiced what we today would call meditation, and they were strict vegetarians, although the eating of fish was allowed.

The Church's rage was primarily directed toward the largest sect known as the Cathars, although there were many other free-thinking sects, such as the Waldensians, in the cities and towns of this newly urbanized area. In general the Cathars subscribed to a doctrine of reincarnation and recognized the feminine principle in religion. Indeed, the preachers and teachers of Cathar congregations were of both genders. At the same time they rejected the orthodox Catholic Church and denied the validity of all clerical hierarchies as being an official and ordained intercessor between man and God.

In the place of "faith in second hand knowledge," these mystically oriented people insisted on direct and personal communion with the Divine, a spiritual experience apprehended by the individual firsthand. This experience has been called gnosis, from the Greek word for "knowledge". For the Cathars, it took precedence over all creeds and dogma. Given such emphasis on direct personal contact with God—priests, bishops, and other clerical authorities became superfluous.

The next few centuries would be turbulent for the evolution of humanity and thought, with the Reformation coming, along with the rise of nations, exploration, and scientific methods for examining and postulating existence. Retaliations were severe, and great men like Galileo would be placed on trial.

With radiant dispassion, stained glass windows filled the cathedrals of Europe and England, giving sublime testimony to the Church's contention that it alone could dispense the light of heaven and offer it to earth to bless the faithful. The beauty of this bejeweled light, cast upon processions of richly robed princes, and choirs singing angelic chants, was assurance that God's kingdom on Earth was being well tended and reverently celebrated.

While thousands held it in contempt, others of equally great vision saw within the Church a long history of human toil, devotion, and community, which for a thousand years had dedicated their lives to a higher end. Despite jealousy and oppression from orthodox powers, who were completely void of enlightenment, other men and women had found their highest realizations of God through the Church. After all, does God seek permission or faint at the limitation of any vessel, sublime, corrupt, or otherwise?

My research would have been easy, although shallow and imbalanced, if I had only drawn evidence of change from radicals moving against the established order. That is almost a redundant proposition. Only the voices of change **within the cloistered halls** held the key I was looking for, and led me to the doors I needed to unlock. Something had to explain why the sculptor known as "The Joseph Master" dressed the Holy Family in fashionable costumes of the day as they posed on the portals of Reims Cathedra.

The key I was looking for is hidden within the very word: "consciousness." Literally, it means "unity of mind." Despite the vital and valuable contributions of many who oppose existing order, those who facilitate our "unity of mind" are usually the ones that carry our strivings to a higher level. Thus, I found my most profitable research in the lives and words of those who changed orthodoxy from within, by their courage and dedication to consciousness rather than to agendas of reform.

The first was Hildegard of Bingen (1098-1179). Here was a remarkable woman. Though still not canonized, she has been beatified, and is frequently referred to as St. Hildegard. She was a first in many fields. At a time when few women wrote, Hildegard was known as "Sybil of the Rhine." She produced major works of theology and visionary writings. When few women were accorded respect, she was consulted by and advised bishops, popes, and kings. She used the curative powers of natural objects for healing, and wrote treatises about natural history and medicinal uses of plants, animals, trees and stones. She is the first composer of music whose biography is known.

She founded a vibrant convent, where her musical plays were performed. Her story is important to all students of medieval history and culture and an inspirational account of an irresistible spirit and vibrant intellect overcoming social, physical, cultural, gender barriers to achieve timeless transcendence.

Hildegard's life demonstrates a perfect example of how authentic mysticism does not lead to contentiousness, but rather, to transcendence of it. In 1141 she had a vision that changed the course of her life and those who would follow her teaching. A vision of God gave her instant understanding of the meaning of the religious texts, and commanded her to write down everything she would observe in her visions.

"And it came to pass ... when I was 42 years and 7 months old, that the heavens were opened and a blinding light of exceptional brilliance flowed through my entire brain. And so it kindled my whole heart and breast like a flame, not burning but warming... and suddenly I understood the meaning of all the expositions."

Hildegard had no interest in schismatics. Indeed, she wanted her visions to be sanctioned by the Catholic Church, though she herself never doubted the Divine origins to her luminous visions. She wrote to St. Bernard, seeking his blessings. Though his answer to her was rather perfunctory, he did bring it to the attention of Pope Eugenius (1145-53), a rather enlightened individual who exhorted Hildegard to finish her writings. With papal imprimatur, Hildegard was able to finish her first visionary work *Scivias* ("Know the Ways of the Lord") and her fame began to spread through Germany and beyond.

Thus began her composition of some of the most beautiful praises to God ever written. They were true testimonies of her direct experience of Divine Grace. Above and beyond mystical theology, her writings were also filled with treatises on the science of life, natural history, and medicinal uses of plants, understanding not usually acquired except through exceptional insight.

She saw beauty in all things and wrote music and texts to her songs, mostly hymns and sequences in honor of saints, and Mary. She describes music as the means of recapturing the original joy and beauty of paradise. Perhaps this explains why her music most often sounds like angels singing. Perhaps because of this cosmic celestial beauty, her music is undergoing a revival and enjoying huge public success again today.

There is no question that Hildegard had been lifted above the limitations and judgments of her day by some extraordinary elevations of consciousness. There is no prejudice in her writings, and no reference to gender dominance, which is even more remarkable for that day. Hildegard's treatises are also unique for their generally positive view of the female consciousness, expressed literally and figuratively, even to the affirmation of sexual relations and her description of pleasure from a woman's point of view. In all of her writings she uses feminine pronouns in reference to the Holy Spirit.

Rather than elaborate more on my opinion of her writings, here are a few quotations of her work. The reader may directly sense the beauty and rapt passion of being directly in communion with what she saw and heard. The following extracts from her writings are celebrations to the Holy Spirit, which she clearly experienced as feminine:

"I heard a voice saying to me, 'This Lady whom you see is Love, who has Her dwelling place in eternity. When God wished to create the world, He leaned down, and with tender Love, provided all that was needed, as a parent prepares an inheritance for a child. And thus, in a mighty blaze the Lord ordained all His works.'

"Then creation recognized its Creator in its own forms and appearances. For in the beginning, when God said, "Let it be!" and it came to pass, the means and the Matrix of creation was Love, because all creation was formed through Her as in the twinkling of an eye.

"I am Wisdom. Mine is the blast of the resounding Word through which all creation came to be, and I quickened all things with my breath so that not one of them is mortal in its kind; for I am Life. Indeed I am Life, whole and undivided -- not hewn from any stone, or budded from branches, or rooted in virile strength; but all that lives has its root in Me. For Wisdom is the root whose blossom is the resounding Word....

"I flame above the beauty of the fields to signify the earth -- the matter from which humanity was made. I shine in the waters to indicate the soul, for, as water suffuses the whole earth, the soul pervades the whole body. I burn in the sun and the moon to denote Wisdom, and the stars are the innumerable words of Wisdom.

"I am the Supreme and Fiery Force who kindles every living spark....As I circled the whirling sphere with my upper wings (that is, with Wisdom), rightly I ordained it. And I am the fiery life of the Divine essence: I flame above the beauty

of the fields; I shine in the waters; I burn in the sun, the moon, and the stars. And, with the airy wind, I quicken all things vitally by an unseen, all-sustaining life. For the air is alive in the verdure and the flowers; the waters flow as if they lived; the sun too lives in its light; and when the moon wanes it is rekindled by the light of the sun, as if it lived anew. Even the stars glisten in their light as if alive.

"She is Divine Wisdom. She watches over all people and all things in heaven and on earth, being of such radiance and brightness that, for the measureless splendor that shines in Her, you cannot gaze on Her face or on the garments She wears. For She is awesome in terror as the Thunderer's lightening, and gentle in goodness as the sunshine. Hence, in Her terror and Her gentleness, She is incomprehensible to mortals, because of the dread radiance of divinity in Her face and the brightness that dwells in Her as the robe of Her beauty. She is like the Sun, which none can contemplate in its blazing face or in the glorious garment of its rays. For She is with all and in all, and of beauty so great in Her mystery that no one could know how sweetly She bears with people, and with what unfathomable mercy She spares them."

Hildegard's life had barely ended when St. Francis of Assisi, one of the greatest exponents of Christian mysticism, was born. Francis' life was perhaps the highest culmination of medieval thought and reverence for life. We will not go to length in this short chapter to review a life so widely known and easily referenced in other books. It is, however, important to note the pinnacle to which he took the mystical experience, not only in the beauty and intensity of his visions, but also in his devotion to reconciling his direct experiences of God with orthodox perspectives. The highest perspectives of consciousness have no contentions, only expansions of enlightenment and compassion reaching toward the Divine.

All manner of people, in all times and cultures, have been drawn to Saint Francis with great interest and affection. Perhaps that is because of his loving devotion to life in all its forms. However, to see Francis only as the universal friend and the joyous singer of nature is to overlook the larger aspect of his work which explains all the rest -- its supernatural side. Francis was a profound mystic in the truest sense of the word. The whole world was to him one luminous ladder, mounting upon the rungs of which he approached and beheld God. Few lives have been more wholly imbued with the supernatural. Nowhere can there be found a keener insight into the innermost world of spirit where the supernatural and the natural blend so resolved into a seamless whole. He found in all created things some reflection of Divine order, and he loved to admire in them the beauty, power, wisdom, and goodness of their Creator. Francis drew sermons even from stones, and good from everything.

Francis's compassion was not simply the offspring of a soft or sentimental disposition; it arose rather from that deep and abiding sense of the presence of God, which underlay all he said and did. Even so, his cheerfulness was not that of a careless nature, or of one untouched by sorrow. Humility was his ruling virtue. Francis ever truly believed himself less than the least.

Francis was prompt and obedience to the voice of God within him. Perhaps his greatest virtue was a completely surrendered adoration of Divine grace. Among his rewards were many visions of Jesus, culminating in the appearance of stigmata (wounds of crucifixion) on his hands near the end of his life.

And thus, without strife or schism, God's Poor Little Man of Assisi became the means for renewing the Church's heart and generating the most potent and popular religious movement since the beginnings of Christianity. No doubt this movement was socially impelled by all the forces of his time, but it could not have happened except through the grace of his true devotion. It would be difficult to overestimate the effect produced by Francis upon the mind of his time, or the quickening power he wielded on the generations which have succeeded him. As his exquisite spirit passed out into the world it became an abiding source of inspiration. It may not be an exaggeration to say (as many have) that all the threads of civilization in the subsequent centuries seem to hark back to Francis.

Well beyond the Church, the world of art and letters is also deeply indebted to the ardent life of Francis. Prose could not satisfy the saint's ardent soul, so he made poetry. He was not skilled in the laws of composition, but his poetry was the beginning of what found its highest expression in Dante's "Divine Comedy". What he did was to teach a people accustomed to the stilted verses of Latin how to use their native tongue in simple spontaneous rhymes and hymns. Further supporting the spirit of his age he wrote the first mystery-play we hear of in Italy, the

"Stable at Bethlehem." Well beyond his own creations, Francis's life inspired the birth of Italian art. His story became a passionate tradition painted everywhere with delight. Full of color, dramatic possibilities, and human interest, the early Franciscan legend afforded the most popular material for painters since the life of Christ.

Through Francis we see once more that great vitality of human consciousness—thrusting forward—finding its power and stimulating the imagination of one who would rekindle a bridge between heaven and earth. Less than three centuries into the future Copernicus would envision such a bridge between our planet and the cosmos, and thereby would begin the scientific revolution.

Before the paradigm changed forever, while perceptions of life were still innocent, two other persons of heroic consciousness emerged to offer us a portrait of heaven touching Earth through human faith. The first was Saint Joan D'Arc, born in 1412. Her innocence, not only as a child, but as a devotee of the highest level to which a soul could ascend, creates an unforgettable portrait of true faith cast against a stagnating dogma that claimed faith as its pillar of authority while persecuting many of those who had indeed attained it.

Like Francis and Hildegard, her life is a stunning illustration of consciousness transcending oppression instead of opposing it. To the end, Joan's faith in God was unshakable, as well as her faith in all of the instruments of Divine connection to earth, even if error and corruption had darkened their vision. Like Jacob had seen his ladder reaching to heaven, she knew her connection would be found through the highest and best within her, not as vanity, but as utter surrender to the force of Grace leading her beyond anything she could personally envision.

A peasant girl born in Eastern France, Joan led the French army to several important victories during the Hundred Years' War, claiming she had visions from God in which explicit instructions were given. She was indirectly responsible for the coronation of King Charles VII, captured by the English, tried by an ecclesiastical court, and burned at the stake by the English when she was only nineteen years old.

For four centuries Joan of Arc's religious visions and her military victories have been told and retold in song, story and movies. The consensus among scholars is that her faith was sincere. Analysis of her visions, however, is problematic since the main source of information about them is the trial transcript in which she defied customary courtroom procedure about a witness's oath and specifically refused to answer every question about her visions. We do know that her first vision happened around 1424 at the age of 12 years when she was alone in a field and heard voices.

Her opponents were primarily motivated by political ends. It is also clear from comments and records that they were deeply afraid of the popular loyalty that Joan had inspired, led, and symbolized. Upon her arrival at Chinon the royal counselor cautioned, “One should not lightly alter any policy because of conversation with a girl, a peasant... so susceptible to illusions; one should not make oneself ridiculous in the sight of foreign nations... ”

There have been many medical speculations about Joan’s mental health including schizophrenia and complications from tuberculosis. None of the alleged diagnoses have gained consensus agreement, however. Even though hallucination and religious enthusiasm can be symptomatic of various syndromes, other characteristic symptoms conflict with the known facts of Joan's life.

Besides the physical rigor of her military career, which would seem to exclude many medical hypotheses, Joan of Arc displayed none of the cognitive impairment that can accompany some major mental illnesses when symptoms are present. She remained astute to the end of her life, and trial testimony frequently marvels at her astuteness: Her subtle replies under interrogation even forced the court to stop holding public sessions. If her visions had some medical or psychiatric origin then she would have been an exceptional case.

The trial record demonstrates her remarkable intellect. The transcript's most famous exchange is an exercise in subtlety. "Asked if she knew she was in God's grace, she answered: 'If I am not, may God put me there; and if I am, may God keep me there.'

The fact is, Joan was a mystic in the truest sense, and operated within a religious tradition that believed an exceptional person from any level of society might receive a divine calling. She was the consummate torch bearer at a time of potent change in Europe, and the epitome of a young woman giving birth to a new nation and a new way of seeing our connection to God and the world.

The next year after St. Joan's martyrdom, Teresa de Cepeda y Ahumada was born in Ávila, Spain. She was of Jewish heritage converted to Christianity, and her grandfather was actually condemned by the Spanish

Inquisition for returning to the Jewish faith. She felt drawn to a life of faith, and wanted no part in the political contentions of the day. Therefore, she left her parents' home secretly one morning in 1534, at the age of 19, and entered the Monastery of the Incarnation of the Carmelite nuns at Avila. In the cloister, she suffered greatly from illnesses that were also accompanied by periods of spiritual ecstasy. This would characterize her whole life.

On St. Peter's Day in 1559, Teresa became firmly convinced that Christ was present to her in bodily form. This vision lasted almost uninterrupted for more than two years. In another vision, a seraph drove the fiery point of a golden lance repeatedly through her heart, causing an ineffable spiritual-bodily pain. The memory of this episode served as an inspiration throughout the rest of her life.

Like so many who presented a depth of experience and truth, Theresa was severely censored and restricted by her monastic order. Yet in her isolation, she wrote prolifically and the mysticism in her works exerted a formative influence upon many theologians of the following centuries. She was a most lucid student and teacher of that which she had experienced and believed to be universally relevant.

The kernel of Saint Teresa's mystical thought throughout all her writings is the ascent of the soul in four stages (found in Theresa's "Autobiography", Chs. 10-22):

The first is the "heart's devotion," or that of devout contemplation and concentration, wherein the soul withdraws from external influences. For her this involved devout observance of the passion of Christ.

The second is the "devotion of peace," in which the human will is lost in that of God by virtue of a charismatic, supernatural state given of God, although allowing that other faculties, such as memory, reason, and imagination, are not yet secure from worldly distraction. At this stage, the goal and prevailing state is one of quietude.

The next step, which is "devotion of union", is not only a supernatural but an essentially ecstatic state. Here there is also complete absorption of the mind in a greater consciousness, and only the memory and imagination are left to ramble. This state is characterized by a blissful peace, a comprehension of higher soul faculties, and a conscious rapture in the love of God.

The fourth is the "devotion of ecstasy or rapture," a passive state, in which the consciousness of being in the body disappears. Sense activity ceases; memory and imagination are also absorbed in God or intoxicated. Body and spirit are in the throes of a sweet, happy pain, alternating between a fearful fiery glow, a complete impotence and unconsciousness, and a spell of strangulation, intermitted sometimes by such an ecstatic flight that the body is literally lifted into space. St. Theresa herself was said to have been observed levitating on more than one occasion.

Her scriptural substantiation for this was 2 Corinthians 12:2-3, "I knew a man in Christ more than fourteen years ago (whether in the body I cannot tell, or whether out of the body I cannot tell -- God knoweth). Such a one was caught up to the Third Heaven." Paul, of course, was no stranger to mystical Christianity. His only known meetings with Jesus were in the form of a great light, bodily apparitions, and voices that comforted him and directed his work. There was great harmony between Paul and Theresa. A verse written by St. Theresa, which would most summarize her life and work, could just as easily have been written by Paul: "It is love alone that gives worth to all things." - St. Theresa of Avila

It seems that consciousness responds to our human requests in surprising and often outrageously creative ways. It offers heightened experience and greater meaning, but often with a price. Therefore, we are impelled to ask why those who seek direct union with God (or pursue the Highest Consciousness) so often suffer hardship and even martyrdom? Is there a causal relationship, or is consciousness simply raised and refined by the fires of challenge? This question is pertinent to every pathway of wisdom ever traveled.

The first and most obvious answer stems from the political inconvenience seekers of higher consciousness cause to those who hold the reins of power but not the heights of wisdom. History reveals all too well the tragedy of this conflict in human evolution.

The second part of the answer comes from a deeper appreciation of consciousness itself. Since the eighteenth century, and the rise of science, there has been a prevailing misconception that knowledge and consciousness are one and the same. Today, with the internet making trillions of data bites available, we are even more entrained to believe that consciousness is somewhere "out there" in storage just waiting to be decoded and assimilated by some giant processor. At last, science is maturing from its adolescent idea that logic can explain everything if given enough information. The most advanced scientists today are cautioning us to realize that we co-create every perception and conclusion from the means we use to observe, measure, and relate to it. They're going so far as to admit we make our highest observations from the incidents of greatest connection with our objects of study. In other words, there is no "out there" and absolute objectivity is an intellectual myth.

It would take volumes to cover all the research available today on the subject of consciousness, and even if it could be briefly summarized, it is not our purpose here to try and define a subject which seems to have its greatest power in **defining us.** Indeed, our pivotal accomplishments, both personally and historically, seem always to be those we might call "defining moments," whether they come from scientific discovery, humanitarian relief, athletic achievements, artistic creation, or the heights of mystical rapture. The content of consciousness seems to be irrelevant compared to the greater importance of how it reaches beyond any known or conventional explanations and then transposes itself into some new form of understanding.

Another salient characteristic of consciousness is that it flourishes in a state of disciplined surrender to whatever is already known or possible. Those who ran a mile faster did so by first achieving the fastest known record to date. Albert Einstein did not abandon the laws of Isaac Newton before his discovery of relativity. Indeed, he was an accomplished mathematician who had examined every possibility within the known universe. His higher discoveries emerged as a transcendence of all the limitations of past thinking. Saint Joan did not abandon theological beliefs that were skeptical of her visions and eventually betrayed her. She accepted everything, and transcended to both military and spiritual glory.

The real point, I believe, is that consciousness is not learned. It emerges spontaneously, often among the innocent, as a manifestation of where the leading edge of human evolution is appearing. Consciousness seems to be the very fire of life moving forward, and it demands surrender of vanity as sternly and it requires a complete symbiotic engagement with all the forces of life. When consciousness reaches beyond existing explanations of "what is," what emerges is the mysticism of creative revelation. Mysticism is simply mystery plus consciousness in creative display of what cannot be otherwise seen or known.

This higher faculty is an amazing affirmation of what many enlightened ones have taught us: namely that the highest component of human nature is that our lives are collectively and personally sculpted entirely from our consciousness.

The first three centuries of Christianity were extremely mystical, in the sense of directly "knowing" from Divine revelations. In Greek, this attitude of devotion was called Gnosis. Many scholars have attributed the origin of these practices to Eastern influences, knowing that mysticism has always been more honored in Asia than it has been in the West. Frankly, I think theories about outside influences on mystical thought are something of a distraction from understanding the true nature of a mystical experience. My scholarly and personal experience over the last forty years has led me to a firm conclusion that works for me. Wherever there are human beings, innocent or sophisticated, who have a demand for growth or change that exceeds the current resources of knowledge or ability, consciousness will strike a new course with visions never seen before! These visions may be religious, scientific, economic, ecological, or projected into realms not previously visited! This is true for all life, but most evident within humanity.

I once owned a vineyard. It was a wonderful place and time that brought many lessons as well as pleasures. One of those lessons, difficult to grasp at first, is that the finest crops were those that were stressed for the last month before harvest. Even in the hot dry Texas summers we had to summon the courage to turn off all irrigation and all feeding for thirty days before the grapes were mature. This forces the vines to find their water and nourishment from the earth, to reach for the sun, to sink their roots deeply, and then create alchemical works of art from their own symbiotic link between heaven, earth, and nature. As a parable of the vine, I think this goes a long way toward explaining the intimate link between challenge and the evolution of consciousness, and how it must emerge from the smelting pot of inescapable transformation, unlike the acquisition of knowledge that can be acquired leisurely in a laboratory or gentleman's study and debated at length over a five-course meal.

Whatever is most vital to our survival does not come cheaply or without our complete obedience to its demands. It may be that the power of consciousness, which brings our immersion into the highest and best we can perceive, does not permit a victory that can be easily dismissed.

Another lesson I learned on the vineyard was the paradox of loving so tenderly a vine that sometimes had to be pruned with unreserved finality. A vine that had been overproducing for so long that its very constitution could be weakened by more production had to be pruned back to the trunk. Vines that were not producing enough had to have their unproductive branches removed until a productive one shot forth. Crops were estimated and carefully controlled for as many as five years before optimum production could happen. What took place in the dormant season was also critical, in fact more vital to production than months of verdant growth. One of the most profound observations I made was my own symbiotic fusion with the vines at the point of consciousness where I knew what to do for their well-being. What I sensed in return was their trust in my decision. There were no reservations about life, merely a full thrust forward to flourish in a new direction.

The vineyard was a university of life. Indeed, in the ancient world it was customary, if not required, for the eldest sons, destined to inherit estates or positions of leadership, to manage the family vineyard in his youth. We see this in the life of David, Solomon, and Jesus, and the princes of Egypt, to name a few. It was as essential to their education as an MBA would be today. I'm sure there was a practical value to their service as well; but, after owning and caring for a vineyard myself, I am also certain there was a much higher lesson about the stewardship of life and the care of not just one but many vines, learning the difference between surviving and thriving, and seeing a vineyard thrive for many future generations.

No doubt, this is why Jesus used the vineyard so frequently in his parables. In the cultivation of its fruit, there is a complete and living symbiosis, from the caregivers, to the soil, to the sun and rain, not to mention the flora culture around it, the aphids, and bees. This is what makes it all a work of art, love, vision, and faith. For the vine this results in wonderful and bountiful fruit.

In retrospect, medieval times seem like a world of fantasy and legend. However, I believe the same faculty that gave visions to Joan before her military campaigns is the same power that still inspires every artist, leader, or scientist who dares to dream of a reality before it is proven to be true. What most symbolically links me with that age is an image of the great rose window of Notre Dame de Paris. I can almost see it turn like a giant kaleidoscope in my mind's eye, reminding me that while all things of the external world change, there are constants within our being and within the universe..

From a modern perspective, what can be said about the reality of mystical visions? Linear time and skeptical beliefs would tend to dismiss them as some form of delusion under duress. In many cases, however, that was far from likely. Like any other action or human creation, we must judge it by its fruit! Perhaps the true standard for reality lies in the quality and mastery of consciousness itself rather than in the content we think is prevailing under a particular set of conditions.

When I accepted the task of researching how medieval thought and expression were transformed by popular culture, mystical and creative geniuses, and the inevitable defense of resistive forces I had no idea where it would all lead. It could have taken a lifetime to complete research on that one topic, but I had gathered enough in two years to write my thesis. I presume it is still filed on the shelves of Tulane University Library along with all the other Master's thesis and Doctoral dissertations of its graduates.

In those two years I was transformed by the amazing lives and events I studied. Before, I was primarily interested in my own creations. By the time I left, I had been introduced to the very process of creation that moves us all. The light of ancient cathedrals would continue to cast its jeweled color on my life. As it would come to pass, God and my own higher consciousness would not be satisfied with anything less than a direct experience akin to what I had read on the pages of history.

Chapter 4

Gunnar Glowstar

Life is uplifted by the love of one pure soul...

What you are about to read is a true story: the story of Gunnar Glowstar. It began on a vineyard in Paradise. ...Paradise, Texas, that is. To Gunnar and me it was simply Heaven.

These were special years, seemingly not on any clock or map. Who would imagine a vineyard in Texas? And yes, it was a real vineyard with all the work, romance, and creative finesse demanded by any vineyard on any slope under the sun. What an education this would be in working with the art and mystery of the vine, which in so many ways summarizes the art and mystery of life. What I learned is beyond estimation, and much of it I learned from Gunnar.

I must tell you about him first, because any story worth telling comes from the voice of love, and love is in the very nature of our being, both man and beast. Gunnar came to be with me in the fall of 1987. Harvest was over, and the glow of autumn had arrived. My own thoughts turned to play, and memories of childhood. Raking leaves, I would remember my younger days when huge piles of them would become landing pads for jumping from low slung tree branches. In that reverie I was struck by an overwhelming desire to adopt a kitten for my playmate. At first it was a pleasant yearning, but soon it grew into a dedicated purpose. I could almost see a particular kitten in my mind's eye with long hair and blue eyes. The more I thought about it, the more I began to realize it was, indeed, a very particular cat who was possibly seeking me as much as I it.

My first course of action was to call all of the animal shelters within about a hundred miles. What if I were receiving messages from a kitten in trouble? I found none fitting that description on first call, so I sent search and rescue letters to all the shelters, and placed an ad in the newspaper, asking for any long-haired cat with blue eyes that might turn up.

Two weeks passed, and I almost abandoned the idea. Maybe some other fate had befallen the cat I was supposed to find, or so I told myself—until, one night, I met him in my dreams! In that dream I was embarking on a long and treacherous climb up a high mountain, one which had been scaled by only a few. It would be my job to blaze a trail and make the pathway easier for others who would follow. In this journey I traveled very lightly and was led only by a great light that glowed around a high created peak. Interestingly, I had one companion—a cat. In my dream I couldn't tell what color he was for he was transparent like a crystal. On the trek he nestled in my knapsack, but he would stand with me at the beginning and end of every day to decide on the trail and take note of what we would be seeing. All I could tell about him physically is that he had long hair and eyes like blue topaz.

The next morning I was renewed in my mission to find him, although a bit mystified by the dream. I checked with the shelters first, but nothing. So I picked up the newspaper classifieds for lost and found. Nothing! Finally, I looked through cattery listings for long-haired breeds. I called them all, and only one prospect emerged. Cathy was the breeder's name, and she explained in a slightly embarrassed tone that she had one eight-week old male that fit my description, but (was quick to add) she could not offer registration for him because he was, well, different. What did she mean by 'different'? I queried? "Oh, he's healthy and happy," she explained. "It's just that his mom and dad were champion Himalayans and he's not up to the standards of the breed. He has a leonine face instead of the flat Himalayan profile, his paws are large, and his body is long. He has a broad chest with full mane and hips so narrow he swaggers when he walks. Actually, he looks like a tiny white lion. These things should make him quite strong and athletic, though." He'll be a great companion. It was him, I knew, and I couldn't agree more that he would be a great companion.

Heaven was speaking, but what was it saying? In the next two years it would tell me more than it had in all previous years of my life. The messages would come from nature and the rich array of life that filled the vineyard. Gunnar would be the master of ceremonies, and I would open my eyes and ears to dimensions of reality I had not directly known in any manner before.

I'm getting ahead of my story, though, and Gunnar would not like that. He wanted to see life in its pure essence every moment, as if it had never been experienced before. I think the Creator gave him those bright blue eyes so that he could see more clearly and reflect back to life all the light he had gathered up. Every moment was new and full of wonder.

If the story were told from his perspective, and of course it also is, I think it would read somehow like this:

Gunnar's mother had gone on her morning stroll, while her little boy amused himself with drapery pull strings and thought about how, just yesterday, he had raced up that towering wall of fabric and found himself perilously perched on top of a slender curtain rod. He remembered how he had to think about every placement of his claws as he backed down the vertical precipice of shimmering cloth. Snags were of no concern to him. They were handy landmarks for a return trek up the high road to adventure. He did not see this experience as one to be feared in any way. Indeed, it would be the beginning of a life-long pursuit of high places.

Yes, he would definitely do that again, but for now it was more appealing just to snuggle under a sofa and catch a few winks. There was something about this day that made him sleepy and disinterested in his usual games. Gunnar drifted into the land of dreams and visited far off places that only his heart remembered. Suddenly he was startled into the reality of this world by a loud bell. Usually that meant that someone was at the door. "Maybe I'll be ignored," he told himself as he maintained a cat-napping pose.

The human who cared for his mom and dad opened the door and began talking with another woman standing in the entrance. Their interchange seemed friendly, which was all that mattered to Gunnar.

Much as he practiced indifference, it did not come easily to Gunnar, and there was something about this conversation that sparked his curiosity. "Are they talking about me?" He winced and tucked in his whiskers.

With every word, he could feel his heart racing faster. It was always exciting and a little scary when humans noticed him. Torn between looking and hiding, he crouched further under the sofa for a moment. Then fascination compelled him to extended one whisker at a time until at last one little blue eye popped out to view the room.

Cathy, the person he had known since birth caught the motion and flutter of white fur. With a quick and certain gesture of caring affection, she swept the little one into the palm of her hand. How undignified it felt to be hoisted in mid-air with four legs dangling!

In a moment this would change. With the innate composure and grace of a dancer, he repositioned himself into a stately and handsome display of miniature nobility. There he reigned in her open hand with sparkling blue eyes flashing while a white plume tail swung gingerly with excitement.

Cathy gestured with the kitten and said, "Here he is, Glenda. This is the little male I told you about, and he's the only one left in the litter. Like I explained, he's different. Now you see what I mean."

Oh, yes, this was the one. What I didn't expect to see was such majesty looking back at me. My instant thought was, "Is there a kingdom where cats rule, and this is a young prince?"

Little Gunnar looked at me with thoughts that seemed to convey: "I saw her in my dreams. I wonder what this means."

Gunnar, posing to conceal the quivering pink nose and nervous hips, chose to find the best angle for leaping back to the floor. But, he paused first. It was clearly a moment of destiny, and his little heart was torn between the life he would be leaving and the new one beginning. His brave facade melted into little trembles and anxious meows as he curled in my hands for the first time.

Such courage and tenderness, bravery and discretion, and above all, alertness to the moment would mark Gunnar's character for all his life.

At that moment all I could think about was how tiny and weightless he was—like a white feather that could blow out of my hand. I asked Cathy if he was a runt or in any way unhealthy.

"Oh, no," she said. "Most Hemys start off small and grow up very slowly. But there's a big spirit inside. You should see him play and stand off the adult cats. It would be them you would worry about!" That was my final confirmation. He had courage and a great sense of play.

As Cathy had foretold, Gunnar took his time growing up, and had a rich and extended kitten hood climbing through thick and winding grape vines as he stalked butterflies and spied on young rabbits or quail venturing from their nests. There was no aggression in him, however, and hunting had no appeal. Life was not a battleground for Gunner, but a playground that he enjoyed to the fullest. This would soon be confirmed as his chosen way of being.

He was such a pure soul he saw everything in life as another opportunity to experience and learn. Life had no end of pleasures. Marigold buttons were just balls to bat in the wind, and leaves floating down from trees were kites to capture and pin to the earth. He saw more than I did and soon he would find a way of sharing that with me. But first he had to teach me about faith.

By his first spring Gunnar had graduated from climbing curtains and shelves, and began to scamper up the tall and spreading oak tree in our back yard. Like all cats he would test for safety and learn as he progressed. At first he would climb up eight feet or so and then retrace his path back a short distance and dive-bomb into a cushy bunch of monkey grass around the tree trunk.

With an agile mind and limber body, he was an acrobat of the first order. He defied consequences as if it were his duty to brush aside the boundaries of normal life. If there was an unusual solution, Gunnar would look for it. His faith in life summoned the inevitable answer to whatever confronted him. Often, I believe, he actually sought for greater and greater challenges just to confirm his certainty about life.

One day he must have been propelled by destiny to do just that. It was the first of many extraordinary things I would witness him do. I was looking out my laundry room window when I saw my little friend gather up the steam of a locomotive heading for the oak tree from twenty feet away. He hit with such a bounding assault that he bolted without pause to the highest branch on the furthest limb. Little though he was, the limb bent with his weight and swayed in the breeze. He just tightened his claws and swung with the motion. His exhilaration was palpable. There he was, out on a limb on the highest place he could imagine! Gunnar was one with life, and the rhythms of nature filled his heart with spaces leading into forever. Through empathy, I could see and feel it.

My more practical feelings took over, however, and I dashed to the back yard to be there for him. Hopefully coach him through the danger. I had no idea he would be coaching me into faith. All kinds of feelings transfer from one to another among friends. Just as I had the thrill of feeling his silky sensations of gliding in the wind a moment before, he now felt my fear for him. Only at that moment did Gunnar realize that he had a problem. How would he get down? Turning around would mean losing his grip, and the leaves and twigs rubbed his backside as he tried to edge to safety in reverse. This could be real trouble and he had no precedent for solving it. He looked at me thirty feet below and bellowed a cry bigger than life. This was the first time I ever heard my little lion roar, and roar it was! He was commanding a solution to appear.

In hopes of providing that solution I ran to the tool shed to grab our tall extension ladder. He was way too far out on a limb to reach directly, but I hoped to climb high enough to call him back to the trunk. Even though he surely felt anxiety in my voice I was urging him to stay calm in soothing tones. Unfortunately, I had confirmed his fears with my own, and added to that, was my momentary disappearance and return with a rattling, clanking ladder that I was lengthening up into the tree. No doubt, he was glad to see me again and to know that someone cared enough to share his predicament. Nevertheless, it was all too strange.

My ascent up the tree must have taken him by surprise. Up to this point, he was the official tree climber in the family. I climbed the ladder up to the first level of forked branches and then ascended up from there in a fashion more like Gunnar. I could see in his eyes that I had successfully distracted him from the fear of his precarious perch, but had replaced it with a growing concern for what I was up to. Our empathy had become so close, I could not mistake his thought that now we might both be in trouble.

Gunnar's imagination was flooded with uncertain impressions. Maybe my ideas would work but they were not appealing to him. All he could see were images of losing his grip, edging backwards through unseen branches, far above ground and safety. He knew I was trying, but what if we failed to make a connection? What if I fell and it would all be his fault? There must be another way.

Just one more roar, and his whole disposition changed from fear to courage. He called up all the memories he had of life confirming faith. What if he pushed it one step further? He had seen squirrels leap from the highest branches and birds launch into flight. Why couldn't he? It would be exciting to try something new and much better than fear!

With the sudden spring of a gymnast, Gunnar jumped from his swaying parapet, extended his legs like the prongs of a kite, and glided thirty feet to the ground. As I watched I turned whiter than his fur, and clinched the ladder as he sailed by in midflight.

He was so engaged with the sensation of doing something extraordinary for the first time, he forgot to be tense. So naturally, a safe landing took care of itself, especially with monkey grass for a landing pad. Quicker than I could balance myself on the ladder and look down, there he was looking up at me and proffering a little meow for me to come down safely.

Gunnar never caused harm to another as far as I know and his behavior was not motivated by fear, which was a rich combination of virtues. Once I watched him guard a baby bird that had fallen from its nest while momma bird dove in swoops trying to drive him away. Of course, momma was doing what nature told her to do, while Gunnar was also providing real safety from potential predators. On his second birthday I decided on a present for him that would either confirm his innate pacifism or provide the stimulus for some aggression therapy that might be wanting. Either way, it would tell a story.

Gunnar was introduced to the next member of our family. This was Alexander, the white mouse. In keeping with the rightful order of nature and the fact that it was Gunnar's birthday present, I introduced them by presenting Alexander inside his little cage with the door open. That way if Alexander was afraid, he would have a safe harbor and Gunnar could express his intentions as nature directed. I had not decided what I would do if

Alexander needed more protection, but instinctively I was not worried. Gunnar was intently curious with his nose to the open cage door. The amazing thing is that Alexander had no more fear than Gunnar. He smartly walked up to the cage door, and pink nose to pink nose they regaled each other with innocence and wonder. Alexander exited the cage and proceeded to give Gunnar a complete sniff-down, and Gunnar him. What a pair they made! I suppose there was some ritual to this, for when it was finished Alexander made a sharp move and a race was on.

Havoc reigned in the living room for a minute or so until a surprise ambush, well-rehearsed from many assaults on falling grape leaves, brought Gunnar into the victor's position with foot on mouse and ready to claim the spoils of war.

The game had been fun, but its conclusion was all too inappropriate for Gunnar. Gunnar groomed life to look good on him, the way most cats groom their whiskers. And, this did not look good or feel good to him, so in a masterful change of pose—forfeiting nothing in the way of pride—he collapsed into a sprawl of utter relaxation. With claws still curled around Alexander he pulled the little creature into his chest. They both curled up to sleep, almost indistinguishable from each other, and that was the beginning of a long friendship.

There are so many Gunnar and Alexander stories, I could write a book on that alone, especially the time Gunnar rescued Alexander from certain downing in the toilet from a miscalculated landing during chase and play.

Soon, however, there was a necessary transition in their relationship. Mice grow up quickly, and I had concerns that Alexander might find a mate and start a family. That would have been all too much! So later that fall, we made him a home with rags and twigs in a corner of our tool shed. He and Gunnar could still play when Gunner was outside. What a sight. Gunnar would head to the door as soon as breakfast was over, and often Alexander would be waiting on the back porch for him. Together, they would stroll to the vineyard for their new day of observing life.

In a sweet and uncanny way, Gunnar had given me a premonition of how a lamb and a lion can peacefully coexist in the chain of life. His gifts to me were, and continue to be, endless.

These were magical days for Gunnar Glowstar. Time was suspended here in the vineyards of Paradise. Nature was rich and joy was abundant. Gunnar grew into adulthood in a place where the choice of "how to be" was always his. He and I gave to each other something that is only shared by true friends. That is the right to be who you really are and the opportunity of exploring the full measure of it all together.

Each new day was a story waiting to unfold. More than anything else, he taught me how to define my days and live within the true nature of time and space. For him day did not begin with dawn or end with sleep. His day began with the announcement of his presence and unfolded with exploration and discovery of the jewels hidden within each moment. As the day mellowed and completed, he would retrace his path through the day's events, pausing to remember or examine the nature of what had happened from a completed perspective. Then he would enjoy his only ritual, the same one he used to greet the day. He would chant! It was a haunting combination of a song and a lion's roar, usually lasting from five to ten minutes.

Space was vast and multi-dimensional in his world. If God has many mansions, I'm sure by now Gunnar has visited them all. Space was precious to him, and was not fixed by form and substance. It was the extension and connection between memories and new possibility. He never ate or slept in the same place, or walked the same path in the same way or time of day. Over the years of living with him it was clear that he never forgot one moment. He would pause in mid-stroll and reflect upon other events that had happened before, where he now casually passed through. He would inventory the completions of his life the way a librarian would inspect her books and fit them neatly on a shelf for future reference. He would try to fit into shoe boxes he had long outgrown, check out all the scents in the storage room where old items of his youth were resting in their own cluttered morgue. He would try to walk on tiny ledges and high shelves that betrayed his adult size but gave meaning and remembrance to his soul. Everything was of one piece. Yesterday, today, and tomorrow were all here in one united place.

Whenever he would join me in the vineyard, it was so easy to extend my perceptions and see into dimensions of reality I normally would not enter. As any good vineyard keeper would to, I studied growth and production needs of the vines, but with Gunnar's help I also learned to see their living essences. The energy they exuded and drew from the earth almost had a song. Gunnar taught me to look beyond the obvious.

One day we were swinging in a hammock overlooking the vineyard when we had a spiritual 'conversation' of major significance to me. I believe it was Gunnar, or at least he helped to facilitate this stream of thought. I was meditating, and he was purring in my lap, when these words came pouring through. "It's easy to go anywhere you wish with anyone you love once you know the difference between space and distance. Distance is just the measure of separation between things and people. Space is all there was before there was matter and distance. Anything can be explored and experienced once distance is gone and all we see is unity. The only reason we see so little is because of the distance we put between our self and others."

The little sage would touch my life deeply, and this was only the beginning. Every day he was stretching my perceptions and teaching me about the power of faith, which is perhaps our strongest connection to God. We were already on our trek up the mountain together. He knew it, and I was learning to notice.

I truly believe that our destiny does not lie in the external panorama of events but in the heart of our own being. To Gunnar, the rightness and meaning of life lays within the heart of the one who lives it. Most certainly it is not to be found within the conclusions we draw about events after they happen, or the embellishments we add in order to make our memories better or worse that they really were.

The summer of 1989 rolled out like a carpet of flowers as we savored life in our private wonderland. Soon enough we would bid farewell to this safe haven as we both moved into a new chapter of our life and inches closer to our chosen destiny. The spirit of life and nature had been our teacher, our guide, and our inspiration. A foundation had been set which could not be shattered by challenges yet to come or higher revelations that would follow. Indeed it would be fulfilled.

Only in retrospect can I see that nature had offered me a direct experience of mysticism much as it had St. Francis. Francis's simple, childlike heart fastened onto the thought that if all creatures are from one Father then all are real kin; hence his custom of claiming brotherhood with all manner of animate and inanimate objects.

On the vineyards of Paradise I had been led into personal communion with Francis' idyllic picture of beasts and birds all being conduits for the presence of God. I could now FEEL his words when he told of how the hunted leveret sought to attract his notice; how the half-frozen bees crawled towards him in the winter to be fed; how the wild falcon fluttered around him; how the nightingale sang with him in sweetest content in the ilex grove at the Carceri, and how his "little brethren the birds" listened so devoutly to his sermon by the roadside near Bevagna; how he delighted to commune with the wild flowers, the crystal spring, the friendly fire, and to greet the sun as it rose upon the fair Umbrian vale.

Legend has it that St. Francis on his death bed thanked his donkey for carrying and helping him throughout his life, and his donkey wept.

I now had my friend, who would travel up the mountain with me and be watchful of my heart. I knew before it happened, there would be much to share and much to remember.

Chapter 5

The Lamb and the Lion

When the short day is brightest, with frost and fire,
The brief sun flames the ice, on pond and ditches,
In windless cold that is the heart's heat,
Reflecting in a watery mirror
A glare that is blindness in the early afternoon.
And glow more intense than blaze of branch, or
brazier,
Stirs the dumb spirit: no wind, but Pentecostal fire
In the dark time of the year.

T.S. Eliot, from Little Gidding

Most epic stories begin long before we know they have sprouted into life. The exact moment when an idea germinates or a passage of destiny begins may be overlooked until the clarity of hindsight can illuminate the dimness of foresight. This is certainly true in the case of my story. If I were to select a critical moment of inception, it would have to be a day of heartbreaking irony, Christmas 1989.

That winter brought to north Texas a wave of bitter cold. Though it would not be a white Christmas, the arctic air would keep our family close to the hearth on Christmas Eve, warming our hands and hearts by the fire.

We retired early, in anticipation of the coming day and fun it would bring with family and friends. Midnight passed, and dawn would soon be arriving. For us, however, there was a different light about to burst on the horizon. At two o'clock in the morning my cat, Gunnar, tore us from the depths of slumber with a siren-like scream. It was not, however, to announce the landing of Donner and Blitzen on the roof. He was warning us that something far more sinister had arrived through a construction flaw in the chimney of our wood-burning stove. Fortunately, Gunnar provided the smoke alarm that was missing in our country home. By that time, fire had consumed most of the living room. Flames and billowing smoke blocked every normal exit from the split-level structure. Our only chance for survival was to jump out of a second story window with a few clothes in hand. We all found safety, but soon our possessions would be reduced to ashes.

On Christmas Day our only solace came in sleep. We had been slumbering for several hours when I was startled from my dreams with a gentle nudge in the ribs.

"Wake up, Honey!" Less than twenty-four hours ago I had suddenly been awakened on the brink of disaster.

"What now?"

Though barely above a whisper, my husband's voice was brimming with excitement. "I just had a dream that you are going to paint a great portrait of Christ, and somehow the fire was necessary for that to occur."

"You're delirious," I mumbled, "Go back to sleep." Not impressed that his dream could be a divine message, I told myself that he was feeling the prayers and sympathies of our friends. I pulled up the covers and returned to my private retreat.

The magnitude of loss was something I would not be able to replace or even confront for many months, much less in the midst of my own dreamland escape from that smoldering catastrophe. Nevertheless, a benevolent glimpse of destiny had been offered as relief from the pain of disaster. This would not be the last message.

More than a year would pass before I could anything paint again. Even then, I noticed that something had changed in my heart. The passion and life of my lost works seemed to belong to days gone by, and could not be generated or sparked by creative impulses in the present. The thought of rebuilding my collection merely for commercial purposes left a dull ache in the center of my being. It seemed that my best option was to proceed on faith and just get busy using the talents I had cultivated for most of my life. Perhaps there would be a surprising new development.

There were no staggering breakthroughs of originality or technique, although my new work was appealing in its own way, and it did have an excellent chance of competing successfully in the marketplace. With that hope in mind, I decided to debut my new work in the fall of 1991 at major dealers' show in Los Angeles. The five-day show resulted in some good orders and a number of promising gallery affiliations, although it was not an overwhelming success by any means. Moreover, I found myself disheartened by an unfamiliar and anxious feeling. For the first time it seemed as though I was conforming to a segment of the artistic world primarily devoted to establishing name recognition by volume production and commercial success. I had been loath to refer my talents to that standard before. Definitely, something had changed.

My criteria for success had always been professionally, academically, and classically sound. After all, my work had been acquired by some of the world's leading museums, and I had been awarded major solo exhibitions. As a portraitist, I had produced portraits for many prominent Americans, including the President pro tempore of the U.S. Senate. My portrait of Dr. Paul Peck was hanging in the Smithsonian Institution, while another of my paintings was hanging in the Museum of the City of New York. A New York publisher distributed my prints, and many of my original paintings were in prominent collections around the country. Altogether, my resume reflected talent, success, and real acceptance by the "keepers of excellence" within the art world. So what was this nagging recrimination I had about also achieving commercial success?

The flavor of external pursuit was leaving a bitter aftertaste. Therefore, with a sense of surrender, I resolved to use the rest of my traveling time for personal renewal. If possible, I would locate a "still point" of peace within myself where truer motives could be examined and reestablished.

A detour from the Interstate in Arizona led to Sedona and the beautiful red rock country south of Flagstaff. Though there was no obvious event, something happened amidst those ancient sandstone spires, because the next morning I felt revitalized and confident to handle whatever was to come. There was a sense that things would be different. Just how different, was still to be revealed.

Homeward bound, I listened to the music of Mozart and allowed its beauty to give my soul wings, it was easy to review my life and highlight the things I considered most important. Eventually silence consumed me, and nothing seemed to be of value except the need to arrive at a new beginning. Without consideration of its impact, I turned to my husband and asked, "If I quit painting for awhile, would you mind?"

"No," he answered, "You do whatever you need to do."

What were thirty plus years of hard work, after all? There was an inner confidence that it would either still be there when I returned, or something else would come along in its place. If I had known what it was to be, I might have been less relaxed about the whole matter.

As we drove across the New Mexico high mesa, my sense of relief matched the expansive horizon. There was a peaceful reverie, which brought to mind impressions of incredible beauty. Though I am accustomed to receiving and playing with visual images, these stood out as extraordinary. Gradually, from a soft inner light a beautiful landscape emerged into focus, there were fields sloping down to a lush green river valley; and, on its banks, a tree with a split trunk sprawled under an azure sky with billowing clouds. This was unusual for me, as my imagination rarely turned to landscapes. Its beauty resonated profoundly through my whole being.

The heightened reverie must have been noticeable, because at that moment my husband asked, "What are you thinking about?"

I'm not thinking about anything. I'm looking at a beautiful landscape in my mind's eye."

"Oh." A minute or so passed, then, "Have you given any thought recently to the idea of painting Jesus?"

I was jolted by this intrusion and wondered how my thoughts and visions could have evoked that response.

"That's a pointless question, because I'm not going to take on the project ... for all the following reasons." I continued with "why." My hope was that if I itemized every objection, then at last the whole proposition would finally be dismissed.

I had studied and taught Art History at two Universities, and my area of specialization was medieval European art which was essentially Christian. So I was well equipped to explain that the history of Christian art had derived its pictorial images from theology. It had its own symbolic language, which served as a teaching tool for the illiterate. This formal symbolic language gave life to Biblical stories. Historical facts about the Jesus' life were scanty, and creative inspiration was usually a threat to the boundaries of Church doctrine. A case in point occurred when Michelangelo almost lost his life by taking liberties with the ceiling of the Sistine Chapel. The Pope was a man of theological protocol, and the artist was a man whose vision into eternal realms was untouched by formula.

I knew of no historical descriptions of Jesus, and certainly there were none in the New Testament. For a portraitist, that alone was enough to stop the project in its tracks. Moreover, as a master portraitist, I knew enough about the art of portrayal to respect the intimate relationship between body and soul. In other words, no other man could pose for Jesus and project the right feelings into a painting.

Now, if those objections were not enough, I was adamant that I would not invent a portrayal of him. In the world of imagination, I felt that everyone had an equal right to see him in their own way. Therefore, I was certainly not going to impose my private preferences upon the consciousness of others. With a sense of finality I presented my closing consideration, in hopes of barring the door to any further discussion. "I'll tell you what. **If he shows up for a sitting, I'll paint him."**

Too exasperated to protest any more, I returned to my private world when the strangest thing happened. A visual arrow shot through my mind with a trailing banner on which appeared the words "The Lamb and The Lion." As these words flashed by, sheep appeared in the pasture of my vision, and the large billowing cloud on its horizon became the shape of a lion. Although there was no human form or presence at that time, I was captivated and stunned by a sudden realization that I would, indeed, be painting a portrait of Jesus Christ.

But how? Had I not established all the impossible conditions?

All I could do was consent to give it my best effort. Upon returning home I gave myself three months to research any available material that might support the project. As a start, I re-read the New Testament, which was of little help since it does not contain a physical description of him, although there are some clues that suggested physical attributes. For example, that he was born into the house of David, that he was a carpenter and fisherman, and that he was physically strong enough to carry a massive cross after enduring brutal torture.

Focusing on his livelihood as a carpenter, my study revealed that carpenters of that time were not only skilled in measuring and joining wood for the construction of buildings or furniture. They were often required to go into the forest, fell the tree, and transform it into lumber they could use. Clearly, carpentry of two thousand years ago was a job for a veritable Paul Bunyan of a man.

Knowing that Jesus' family belonged to the house of David, within the tribe of Judah, I studied the recorded attributes of those people. Each of the twelve tribes of Israel had its own character, appearance and domain. Then, as now, genetic potential in Israel was greater than modern stereotypes would suggest. Ten of the twelve tribes disappeared when the Babylonians scattered the Jewish people in the Diaspora (the "lost tribes of Israel" that we often read about). Only the lines of David, Benjamin, and the Levites, along with various remnants of other tribes returned home. From David came the rulers, aristocrats, and military elite of Jewish society, a fact that made them the target of conquerors. In the siege and destruction of Jerusalem, Roman armies and occupation decimated the line of David, leaving the others to carry on.

Centuries later, as medieval Europeans returned from pilgrimages to the Holy Land, they would bring home descriptions of that limited remainder as representing all of Judaic character and heritage. Such reports were often co-mingled with descriptions of Arab and other Middle East people costumed in typical desert attire, so that stereotypes emerged and formed the backbone of oversimplified pictorial depictions that persist even into modern times, most especially in Christian art.

Within the few surviving descriptions of ancient Jews, there are descriptive references to the Tribe of Judah as often being taller than the other tribes, as well as being the "fairest of the fair." When asking my Semitic friends as to the meaning of "fair" in their world, I was cautioned not to assume that it would likely mean blond in the Northern European sense. However, it could include light olive to fair skin with hair ranging from light golden brown to red-brown, and eyes from hazel to blue green.

Although he might have appeared in different ways to different people, the charisma which drew strangers and crowds to him tends to suggest that he was exceptionally appealing by some measure—at least when he **chose to be**! What form that might have taken, I could only guess, and guessing is something that a true portraitist is loath to do. The earliest paintings of him, from the first and second centuries, show a handsome youth, but those portrayals reflected the influence of Roman fascination with Apollo rather than any true likeness of the Nazarene. Often those symbolic parallels came to be exploited and confused as the church was Romanized.

For this reason, early church leaders actually prohibited artists from portraying Jesus in any manner which was physically strong or beautiful. They supported their contention by emphasizing a 700 BC prophecy in the Old Testament book of Isaiah 53:2, regarding the future coming of a Messiah: "(H)e had no form or comeliness that we should look at him, and no beauty that we should desire him." Most scholars today agree that this prophecy cast a forward glance upon the Messiah's **character and leadership demeanor** rather than his physical appearance. In other words, the coming Messiah would not be a worldly prince, rich and well arrayed, from whom one would seek political favors, privilege, and financial advantage. In every way that interpretation would have been true. However, would it not be odd if the Lord of Life who could raise the dead were, himself, anything less than a picture of health and physical well being? To me that logic is inescapable, but to church authority, concerned only with establishing his **spiritual supremacy**, that passage from Isaiah came in handy for diminishing any focus on his physical form. Most portrayals of him in the last seventeen hundred years are a legacy from that theological decision.

The power of tradition was ominous, and the more I knew, the less capable I felt. All the conditions that I stipulated were based on points of integrity, about which I felt strongly. Therefore, it was an impossible scenario. How could I ever do this painting? The many tidbits were interesting, but if I just pieced them together I would have a quilt, not a whole image with character and strength. After three months, every road I traveled led me to a dead end, and the contradictions before me were more than I could deal with intellectually, much less emotionally.

Now, what was I to do with what I had learned? By itself it had no power, application, or validity.

The answer came on November 23, 1991. The lovely autumn day portended nothing but its own beauty. I had no hint what was about to happen, or that it would bring meaning to the discordant affairs of previous years and open windows to an inconceivable future.

Clear morning light spread its fingers across the lawn, brightening everything in its path as it brought into focus a few bright red leaves still clinging to the trees of our large city lot. Such times are made for dwelling in thought, and I had much to think about. Steam from the coffee warmed my face, and the hammock rocked slowly, stirring the cool November air.

Sorting through memories, I rather enjoyed the panoramic flashbacks of personal history. The recurring pattern was clearly one of sudden reversals and new beginnings. If I had understood paradox then, as well as I do now, perhaps I would have looked for prophecy in the reversals of my life instead of contradiction. However, I simply reviewed my thoughts in that clear November light, and found peace in the hammock's rhythmic swing. It seemed to be gently suggesting ... surrender ... surrender ... surrender.

Despite my pleasant reveries, the awesome glow of nature was distracting me from the inner simplicity I needed. Besides, it was time for lunch. After a quick sandwich, I decided to linger in the dining room for meditation and prayer. This room was central to the house, and so when the chandelier was off there was a pleasant half darkness even at midday.

It was a great room in which to be alone with God. My prayer began with protests, pleas, and conditions, which I hoped would vindicate my resistance. Then I expressed my emotions, doubts, and fears. Yet there was no relief. Finally, I asked forgiveness for having considered anything so presumptuous and outrageous. Especially since my relative lack of passion for the project was unworthy of its importance. Still, there was no resolve. Last of all, I considered that my engagement with the idea was merely a stepping stone to some other more sensible undertaking, which was yet to be revealed. Exhausting myself through exploring all the possibilities of what that might be, I finally rested my head in folded arms on the table. For more than an hour I slept.

What aroused me was a brilliant glow in the room. Resplendent and glistening light engulfed my body and being with a new aliveness.

The brilliance was intense. It filled the room so completely that all shadows departed. Glancing upward, I observed the chandelier was off. This was not surprising, because I sensed there was nothing artificial about the soft white radiance infusing everything, like a cloud descended from Heaven. The whole house possessed a stillness and silence of new fallen snow.

Through the quiet, reverent space there streamed silvery threads of light, energetic ripples, and pulsations of air being expanded as if by a flame. The ripples, which flowed in all directions, took their source from a spot of hyper-luminescence that was almost blinding. This resplendence was like a sun, though not fiery. More likely, it was a concentration of the same quality of light that was everywhere. Its special glory was in its dazzling brightness and the patterns of silver and gold, which were laced with opalescent white and sparkles of lavender, blue, and rose.

I could only look toward the center for a second before the light caused my eyes to fill with tears. Stunned, I had to look away, and at that moment I heard sounds forming into the pattern and cadence of language, although it was no language I had heard before. As the "words" formed a meaning in my mind, the message was "Greetings Glenda.”

In this Presence there was unspeakable Holiness. If light could sing, it would have been chanting celestial sounds. If light were fragrant, it would have exuded the innocence of high, mountain air. I turned to look again, but the radiance was completely overwhelming. Closing my eyes, I protected them from the glow and wept at the same time. No sooner had I escaped within myself than this Holy Presence shot a beam of energy from itself to a point between my eyebrows. There was a sensation of pressure, which caused me to open my eyes and verify. What I saw was a stream of energy pouring in. Returning to the comfort of my inner vision, I watched as a picture was being etched into pictorial awareness. It took about five seconds for the rendering to be completed. The vision seemed to be implanted in the optical part of my brain. It was immutable and would be available for me to view whenever I chose.

Mesmerized by its beauty, I gazed in rapture upon an inner vision of Jesus Christ, which was complete, three-dimensional, and holographic. Majestically, he stood on a hilltop overlooking a green river valley, towering above grazing sheep, while a billowing cloud on the horizon was forming the shape of a lion. I couldn't have asked for a more vivid or realistic picture from which to paint. It was the next best thing to actually being in his presence. Interestingly, though, he did not look as any of my preconceptions would have envisioned. Conditioned, as most western Christians are by Semitic stereotypes, I was surprised to be looking into deep greenish blue eyes framed by amber brown hair.

When my awareness finally externalized, I found that the radiant light had gone and objective reality conformed to normal expectations. Nevertheless, I knew that something about me would never be the same again. That intuition proved to be true, for everything in my life changed after that Holy Moment.

Chapter 6

Born of the Light

The splendid light would be forever etched on my soul or perhaps united with my heart in a single, enduring beat. Within me now, a spark of light had been awakened which would become the doorway to greatly expanded awareness and life.

Forty days would pass before this encounter would be secure enough in my three-dimensional life to actually begin the painting. Each morning I eagerly sought to cultivate a conscious relationship with the vision through reverent acknowledgment and meditation. I would study its every nuance, and inhale it into my being like the breath of life. As the days passed, the vision became more complete and the presence of Jesus grew more alive. This alone distinguished it from my past experience with visual inspirations or dreams, which usually diminished with every repetition of memory.

At first, the sensation was like that of peering through a clear window and greeting a friend looking back from the outside. The beautiful eyes entreating my devotion would eventually dissolve the "glass" boundary between us and magnetically draw me into his world. As that happened, his presence was correspondingly more compelling and dynamic. It seems as though I had entered a world of sensory richness as vivid and complete as an epic dream, but this "dream" was in a state more wakeful than any I had ever known. To consider another very relevant contrast, the dreams of our sleeping state are entered through darkness, and my visits with Jesus were entered through a pin hole of radiant light which was both palpable and living.

The days between November 23rd and January 1st were fertile days of creative preparation, explorations of personal reality, and intellectual contemplation, which had suddenly taken a quantum leap into the realm of cosmic and infinite probability. It's interesting how I recalled my years of being on university faculties. As a scholar of Medieval Christian art, I was familiar with many recorded, and often illustrated, paranormal visions of Jesus or Mary. Considering the monastic life of extended hardship and duress, which the recipients often suffered, at first I felt some concern about my own well-being. But glowing health soon dispelled those fears, and my greater fascination turned to another spectrum of my academic background—the study of light and physics. In all of this, I had been given the rare opportunity of having a mystical experience, profoundly vivid to all the senses, at a time in history when enough information exists about the universe to offer insights and bridges to unite the "normal" with the "paranormal."

Our universe has so many known dimensions beyond our familiar three (plus time) that it is now being referred to as a multiverse in most scientific circles. To deny the fact that many dimensions of reality exceed our normal human senses would be similar to maintaining that the earth is flat after sailing around the world. There has also been significant research about the holographic nature of light, which is the constant of our known universe, not to mention the holographic functions of the human brain. Research has conclusively demonstrated that whatever we "see" in the visual cortex was not merely a response to patterns of light, dark, and color, but also to frequencies of various wave forms. Moreover, our brains use the same mathematics as holography to convert those wave forms into discernible images. To push this one step further toward its logical conclusion, it might even be suggested that objective reality—the world of matter, structure and things—may not even exist in the way we perceive it to be. At the very least what we call "reality" could be perceived differently from diverse perspectives and various states of conditioning.

As we learn more about expanded realities, we may find better explanations, which are scientifically plausible, for paranormal phenomena, synchronicities, and the apparently meaningful coincidence of events. One of the great scientists of our time, David Bohm, asserted that all of tangible reality was a kind of hologram, where any part of the whole could not only be found within a vast and primary level of reality, but also could be replicated infinitely from it.

These were awesome concepts to ponder, and never before had they been more relevant to an actual experience, at least not for me. The fullness of that relevance would be affirmed in future events. In the meantime, there were lingering personal reservations and silent anxiety about this sacred subject I would be presenting to the world—**if** my artistic efforts were indeed successful. The word "if" still wafted through my consciousness on occasion, and I would seek corroboration in my every conversation and excursion to the outer world. I shared the vision and its details of green meadows and sheep with my husband. He responded with a suggestion that proved to have both a convincing and "grounding" effect. He suggested that I have some direct contact with live sheep, and perhaps sketch or photograph a lamb to create a more tangible reference point for the painting.

After canvassing every sheep ranch within three counties, we were discouraged by information that late November was an unlikely season for lambs. Undaunted, though we decided to visit my hometown farmer's market on Saturday. Starting at the crack of dawn, with camera in hand, we were off to hunt for lambs. At least if I could hold a lamb and get a souvenir photo, then some progress would have been made.

On arriving, we made a quick dash to the livestock area, only to meet with another disappointment. There had been two lambs, which were already sold by 8:30 that morning. Feeling out of luck, and outside my flow of destiny, I was ready to go home. Then, in the corner of my eye, down another lane, I spied a scraggly flock of mixed breeds being shepherded by a grizzled old migrant dealer. It was an unimpressive assortment of dirty, lumpy, wool-bearing creatures. Once more I started to turn away when suddenly one sparkling white ewe emerged from behind the flock and made her way over to me. I had never seen anything like her short pristine wool, long neck, and regal face. Her stately appearance was only enhanced by her obvious pregnancy.

Spontaneously, I called her Mary, after the nursery rhyme. For her fleece *was* "white as snow." We bonded within minutes, and the urge to adopt was overtaking me. I quickly reasoned that there would soon be a lamb, and therefore, by purchasing Mary I would have them both available for study. The greater coincidence was that our restored farmhouse was zoned for agriculture even though it was nestled within the city. There we were, two rookie city shepherds loading Mary in the back seat of our Cadillac. She still sparkled, even outside her natural environment, which prompted me to ask the dealer about her breed. "She's a mouflon," he answered, as I handed him my check. That meant nothing to me, and so without further conversation we drove away.

We felt a little "sheepish" as people gawked and laughed at our back-seat passenger. But what did they know? To distract ourselves from the embarrassment, we cooed to Mary and made plans for her housing. Then, the question suddenly popped up, "What's a mouflon?" The name was somewhat familiar, but suddenly I was frozen with discomfort that perhaps Mary was one of those new hybrids not yet on the earth when Jesus walked it. I had visited my uncle's sheep ranch many times as a girl, and I had never seen anything like her. The more I thought about it, the more it became an issue, for any modern element would surely compromise the painting's integrity.

After Mary was settled in her quarters, I set out for the library to get my question answered. I found my answer very quickly on the pages of an encyclopedia. In amazement and disbelief I looked for confirmation from two other sources. The mouflon was recognized as the oldest domesticated breed of sheep in Europe, and is considered to be the ancestor of all domesticated varieties. **Moreover, it was commonly herded in the Middle East 2,000 years ago.**

I re-read those passages until they were committed to memory, and with private elation I pondered the miracle of how many parts of the puzzle had to have already been in place for such an amazing act of perfection to occur. Short of traveling to the Middle East and bartering with a Bedouin, I could not have obtained a more suitable sheep to model for the painting. The odds of finding Mary in my hometown were staggering to the imagination. As a child I had played on the very ground where I found her. How long ago, I wondered, was this painting committed to destiny?

There was an irony to finding Mary, in that I took it for a sign of greater solidity and certainty, when actually it was a just another miracle and call for faith advancing toward me. The renowned quantum physicist, David Bohm, once said, "Matter is frozen light." His comment points toward what may be the ultimate paradox of our universe: That which is unfolding before us most certainly was once enfolded from designs and radiance beyond our imagination.

Considering the approach of Christmas and holiday activities, I decided that it would be better to start the painting early in January. Besides, this would give me time to make some preliminary decisions and prepare the canvas. The first thing I needed to establish was the scale. So, I cast my attention on the vision and asked for guidance. This was the first time it ever occurred to me to regard the vision as a means through which to communicate. The answer was clearly given to me in a telepathic mode, though no words were spoken. The canvas was to be forty-eight inches square.

That was a restless December. I felt like a racehorse waiting for the gate to open. Reassuring myself frequently with inward glances, the vision remained crystal clear and seemed to intimate that a whole new world was being born. It was clearly alive, and I beheld it in wonder. It was presenting and magnifying so much of his life force that what started out as only a visual image gave witness to a feeling that "He was there!"

The days grew long and tense, although the sense of communion between us was bursting with excitement and the silence which filled the spaces of my anticipation were rich with words yet unspoken.

On January second I entered my studio with a peace that made for uneasiness...a peace that my body could only recognize as the bristling and imminent presence of destiny. Even though the room smelled not of incense, but of linseed oil and turpentine, it possessed the subtle ambiance of a temple. Perhaps my own feelings were displaying the nature of my expectations. Or perhaps there was a holiness of spirit, which preceded my arrival on that day and had prepared a place for the "opening lines" of the creation to come. Either way, my senses were clear and clean, as if I had been newly born to the world. Everything, from the dust on the windowsill, to my slightly askew arrangement of brushes, to the towering easel in front of me, adorned the moment with details I will never forget. The room was filled with natural sunlight, although it conveyed the sense of another sacred light I had experienced earlier. As I passed through its rays, my body's motion slowed down to time frames that were seconds long and moving toward stillness. I was overcome by the serene inevitability of that moment—as if everything was suspended in time and space. It felt as though a thousand eyes were upon me, and I searched the space within and without to discover my "watcher."

The silence was broken only by a chant of meows outside the studio door. Gunnar, my beautiful cat, wanted to join whatever was happening in the studio. I moved with some reservation toward the door, and hesitantly opened it. Somehow, I expected to see more than Gunnar, but was quite relieved to see only his little blue eyes twinkling up at me. He darted in quickly, as if to suggest that timing and opportunity were essential to the moment. Something was about to happen which was not to be missed. Then he scurried over to one of the two white pillows I used for meditation and prayer.

I turned to face the large pristine canvas mounted on my easel, but I did not yet have the right feeling to begin. So, I joined Gunnar on the pillows and began my daily practice of acknowledging communing with Jesus by focusing on the spot of light within until the vision emerged. Today, especially, I wanted to study its details as closely as possible, because once I switched my focus outwardly toward the canvas, my whole attention would be cast into the creative process. Suddenly, another meow from Gunnar disrupted the intensity of my meditation as a gentle wind swept through the room, brushing my face. The light "within," which had been illuminating the picture in my mind was now shining through my eyelids from **without!** With a certainty unparalleled in my life, I opened my eyes to behold Jesus standing in front of me, towering above my seated position at his feet.

With slow and careful reverence, I arose, took my place in the painting chair, and began to draw on the canvas. The problem of how I could behold the vision and paint at the same time had been solved, although by what power of majesty or mystery, I could not say.

There were no words, but I could not stop smiling as I began to transcribe his presence onto the pure white surface. From that day forward, whenever I worked at my easel, he would appear as if in full living reality, three-dimensionally before me. Day by day, it was more than a vision. He was there, and we would become a team for creating his painting.

It took two or three days to complete the drawing, so I didn't start painting until the following week. Even then I expected the work to move with slow deliberation. The first layer of paint needs some time to dry. Fortunately, some of the colors dry a little faster than others, so there's usually some part of the canvas that can be worked on. Nevertheless, waiting at least one day is typical. The next morning I entered the studio to check on the canvas and *everything* was dry. Absolutely everything! I was shocked. I never use dryers or thinners because the constitution and longevity of the paint could be compromised. So how was this happening? It was a mystery to me, but the fact was, the paint **always** dried within hours (not days) for the duration of this project. That would have a tremendous impact on its estimated date of completion.

The painting unfolded without interruption. The timing of everything was flawless, and all my needs were provided with surprising efficiency.

The daily occurrence of miracles in the midst of ordinary procedures eventually allowed me to develop a new pattern of expectation about the possibilities of life. I began to observe that resistance, problems, and complexities of life were directly related to my belief in certain levels of difficulty—or density—within matter, energy, time, or circumstance. I came to observe for myself that humankind has entered a world more dense and full of conflict and resistance than necessary because our beliefs, conditioning, and agreements have lead us to expect it.

I was also able to observe that when reality expands or elevates into greater possibility, a perceivable field of light accompanies that translation, and there is a sense of invisible illumination beyond that, which cannot be seen. There is no accident that we associate expansions of consciousness with light and our difficulties with darkness.

We usually think of light as glowing radiance from the sun or some other energetic source. However, both physicists and mystics confirm there is a far more elemental phenomenon than the release of photons from the combustion of material substance. Visible light is but a small part of the spectrum of energy, and photons are an aspect of every part of that spectrum. Through scientific measurement we know of many forms of invisible radiation. For instance, radio waves can be picked up from distant galaxies, and the cosmic background radiation throughout the universe may well be fossil light from the "Big Bang."

If we look closely at the "wave function" of light and what happens **between** photon particles, we can see a very strong connection between material and non-material existence—perhaps even a connection between physics and miracles. Albert Einstein exposed a fascinating characteristic of light in that it is both a wave and a particle. This was a necessary distinction, because the wave function can be spread out in space as a probability distribution, but exactly **where it is** cannot be known. Only when it emits radiation, can it be localized. At the moment of action, the whole probability distribution of the wave collapses to a particular point. This two-part nature of light reveals itself almost like a heartbeat. Perhaps the very heartbeat of the universe is the rhythm of light from wave probability to point and back to wave probability again. Not only that, all time and motion cease at the point where any other form of matter or energy approaches or becomes equal to the "speed of light." In that condition all limits of resistance are eliminated. It is also believed that the constancy of light provides an attractor field, which is fundamental to the energetic formation of gravity. If that is true, then we would have to suspect there to be nothing that could not be created, recreated, redirected or halted at the speed of light.

Not only light—but also life—is more fluid than our perceptions normally admit. As the events of our life approach and disappear, space conforms to the needs of a given purpose, and time is simply a loom that weaves the threads of connection and dimension. Events arrive. In a heartbeat they are gone. Light may well be the instrument through which not only normal but also miraculous transformations of time, space, and matter happen—even if their causes are Divine! In the words of Jesus, "I am the way, the truth, and the light."

I witnessed and learned all these things as the painting progressed. The story of this experience and our conversations that emerged within it are all told in my first book, *"Love Without End, Jesus Speaks."* There were many miracles during the two months of its creation, and many that followed.

The painting was finished on March 12, 1992. On that day, there was little left to do. I was down to polishing particulars. I wanted to add a few strokes to his hair. It was blowing in the wind, and I wanted to separate the strands to show a lightness of air passing through it. One after another, I put these final touches in place. When I looked up I was startled to see the vision dissolving into a cloud of sparkling light. Almost in panic, I looked inward to the point where it had been joined to my consciousness, but the connection had been severed. The spark of light that had been the trigger point of translation between our worlds was now diffusing into a field of light and blending with the light around me. Setting my brush down, I smiled, then smiled bigger, unable to suppress the joy I felt. As I beheld the vision departing, I also witnessed a beginning. Although the visual image faded, the love and energy of its essence settled in upon the canvas. The painting was finished, but its life had only begun.

The Lamb and The Lion

Chapter 7

Life Goes On...

This is the use of memory:
For liberation—not less of love but expanding
Of love beyond desire, and so liberation
From the future as well as the past.

T.S. Eliot, from Little Gidding

I was filled with deep contentment and peace; also a twinge of uneasiness. The painting was finished, but not my destiny with it. Soon I would be plunged into a greater unknown. Only days after the painting was finished, I sat before it, reverently remembering the pleasure of his company when a mixture of tears and smiles filled my countenance. Mainly, however, I felt confusion and concern--old familiar feelings I had not known since before the visitation. "Why? For what purpose has this painting come to be? What should I do with it?"

I missed him deeply, though his love was lingering everywhere like the fragrance of clean mountain air. Within a few days, however, my heart was filled again with the soothing resonance, which I recognized as his Presence. A new dimension of our relationship had begun, along with a new and deeper means of communing.

Though no words were spoken, my questions could now be answered.

I **felt** him say with unmistakable clarity, *"Give it to my people."*

He had answered my question, but with no clues of how to proceed. Moreover, his request was easier said than done. His people are everywhere! They come in every color, nationality, and heritage. Within the Christian community there are countless creeds and hundreds of Church denominations. Many of his most devoted students and disciples do not participate in any religious services at all. And well beyond the boundaries of what we call Christianity, his teachings are an influence around the world.

Where was I to begin? The obvious answer was anywhere. With simple, contagious enthusiasm, word began to spread. Soon strangers from across the country would be arriving at the door, unannounced, asking to view the painting of Jesus! It is staggering to imagine how many barriers had to come down, and how many inhibitions had to be suspended in order for such a thing to happen. People became a living miracle as they sought and experienced his presence through this visual presentation. As visitors carried back their reports of excitement, invitations began to pour in for public appearances. In the next two years, the painting traveled across five states to more than eighty churches and most denominations... not to mention the myriad environments which represented no stated belief at all! Reaching well beyond the walls of church dominion, we went wherever we were called.

The dedication I felt toward *"The Lamb and The Lion"* reduced everything else in my life to virtual unimportance. I was so enthralled in the process of sharing, that my painting career lay in abandonment until September 1993.

At last, on that bright, autumn morning, I wanted to create art again. What's more, I wanted to do it in a home that did not belong to the rest of the world. As I recognized my personal yearnings, I recalled the serenity of being in his presence. It was so different from the hectic pace I had been maintaining.

Looking across the living room, I focused upon his countenance in the painting, hoping to join him in that place of special peace. Just then a very interesting thing happened. Instead of seeing his face, I saw hundreds of other faces--people whose lives and hearts had been changed forever by this new reminder of his living presence. One by one, layers of faces peeled away until I saw only his. That communication had special meaning for me. Through this experience of simplicity, reverence, and sanctity, I knew that a turning point had arrived in the life of the painting. Just as I wanted the solitude and sanctuary of my studio again, I was being told that the painting required sanctuary as well. It needed to be in a reverent and quiet place where the hearts, lives, and beliefs of everyone approaching it could be equally respected.

I did not have the answers, although I was certain he did. Through prayer and meditation I released my anxieties to a higher guidance. Sometimes, however, release is easier hoped for than attained. For several weeks, no logical solutions were presented, and worries mounted. I didn't have a clue where to look. Tense days led to restless nights as I continued my outreach and kept up normal routine. I should have expected a miracle, but as usual, it caught me by surprise.

For the second time in my life I was about to be awakened by a holy light in my home. This time it happened at three o'clock in the morning. Startled from sleep, I sat up in bed and cleared my eyes. It soon became evident that the light was supernatural, just as the first one had been. So, I propped up my pillows and waited. Within minutes the light had become focused in the corner of the room, taking the form of an angel. Perhaps the form was only an adjustment of my mind applying familiar patterns and concepts to the undeniable yet unknown presence in front of me.

It was a startling phenomenon! As a child I had believed in angels, although I never thought about them except at Christmas, and certainly I never expected to see one during my years on earth. What was before me was a rare perception that I was unprepared to explain. Even though my lifetime of involvement with the visual arts had assisted me in developing a strong and vivid imagination, until 1991 my perceptions had never exceeded the normal fabric of natural probability. If anyone had asked me to paint an angel, I would probably have responded in the manner of Courbet, the great French realist, who said more than a century earlier, "If you show me an angel, I'll paint an angel." Consequently, my logical demands left me unprepared for what was before me.

Bewildered and stunned, I stared into the light as the angel said, "Don't be afraid. I have come to let you know that your prayers have been heard. Arrangements are being made for the painting's home."

I was delighted with **what** he said, but I was even more fascinated with **how** he said it. The sound that my **ears heard** was lovely celestial music, while at the same time the sound that **my mind heard** was the spoken English language. It left me with the distinct impression that the music he "spoke" was a universal language which would have translated into whatever word-based language anyone hearing it might be accustomed to using. In days to come I would reflect back upon this event. In one of those moments it occurred to me that even though I saw a form made of light, it might have been transduced from a very abstract universal presence to a form more suitable for perception.

His stay felt like twenty minutes, but it was probably shorter than that. No less than the angels of legend, he was the bearer of good news as well as the bringer of answers. Despite my repeated requests, however, he would give no specific details on the "bigger picture". Before leaving, he placed his "hand" on my heart and said "I leave you with this seed of consciousness in which you will find further insight and instructions."

I waited passively under the supposition that any instructions or answers I needed would come forth spontaneously. After a week or so, however, curiosity overtook my patience. Waiting has never been my favorite pose, and certainly not with matters of destiny. I thought of a thousand prayers, but quietly surrendered to silent meditation, hoping to fall into that special place in my heart where the angel had left "the seed of consciousness." I dwelt in peace for the longest time, then looked, knocked and prodded. Nothing came. Just as I was about to leave that contemplative state I heard the music again. I focused in as I had done before, and the words came forth.

"What?" I shook my head in disbelief. The one thing he said made no sense in relation to my concerns. He told me to "build a prayer screen."

What was a prayer screen, and why did I need to build one? I had sought an answer and received a work order! For the rest of the day I searched for justifications, but none of them made any real sense. The only rational conclusion I could draw was that a prayer screen might foster a place of greater reverence in which to pray and meditate more effectively.

Nevertheless, who am I to argue with an angel? Off I went to our local home improvement store to search for ideas of what to build and how to do it. I spent considerable time there walking the aisles, looking for sparks of inspiration and clues of how to proceed. After the many months of renovating our house, I knew my way around rather well and was on a first name basis with most of the employees. In spite of that, my search that day seemed to be in vain. All of the materials were rough and heavy, requiring power tools. On my way out, I was walking down the aisle of doors when suddenly I tripped on a solid object and almost tumbled to the floor. Someone had left a door lying flat on the floor. I reached down to pick it up, expecting it to be heavy. Much to my surprise it was very lightweight. It was a hollow ash door, and as I held it I noticed how lovely the wood grains were. Moreover, it was only twenty-four inches wide--a suitable width for what I needed. Within minutes I was imagining the possibilities. I could hinge three of these panels together and have a lovely screen! A bit of decoration, some varnish, and then it could be a prayer screen--whatever that might be.

The motif of synchronicity and purposeful coincidence was only just beginning. The doors needed to be shortened, but I had learned how to do that from the workmen who had helped me renovate our home. Once the panels were ready to be assembled I took them into my studio. Looking them over carefully I noticed that the grains on one side were beautiful and suitable for varnish as they were. However, all three doors were plain on the other side. Clearly, they needed some enhancement. But what? Before I knew it, I was standing before one of the ash panels with brush in hand, spontaneously painting an angel.

It seemed to be an appropriate reflection of responsibility back to the one who had placed the order. Little did I know that the door in front of me was more than a painting-- it would become a threshold for my own greater unfolding! On that day in the studio, my only known intent or purpose was to decorate a "prayer screen" and complete a work order! For my reward, I hoped to find an answer on the other side of that project. The answer took its time in arriving, but the reward which accompanied it was greater than anything I expected.

To begin with, there was a noticeable upsurge of energy and personal joy as I painted the angels on those doors, and the completed screen was much more beautiful than I envisioned. It was finished just in time to be shown at our annual Christmas party, although it was not for sale. It had been a year since I had presented any new work, so that fact alone made it the talk of the party. There also was something refreshing and candid about the response it elicited. One woman, in particular, fell in love with it and persistently tried to buy it. Uninterested by her proposition, I explained the best I could, that the screen had a special inspirational value to me and that it was not for sale. Disregarding my "No," she telephoned daily until I finally consented to her wishes. Her persuading argument was that I could make another one for myself. With that plan in mind, I agreed that she could have it.

As soon as she arrived home with her angel screen she noticed that it was too large to fit comfortably with the floor plan of her house. Undaunted by small issues, however, she took an imaginative look at another possibility and then telephoned me to gain support for her idea. She wanted to dismantle the screen and hang the separate panels on her wall. In the final analysis, she loved the angels more than the screen. As a result of her influence, new perceptions and possibilities would open for me as well.

Meanwhile, other coincidences, which could hardly be regarded as accidental were happening through her. Two days later she telephoned again, asking me if I would be willing to replace the angel panels she had purchased. "Why," I asked? "Have they been stolen or damaged?"

She timidly admitted that she had sold them, and proceeded to explain why. A prayer group she belonged to had met in her home the night before, and two members of the group wanted to purchase the panels for their church. With a persistence reminiscent of her own, they apparently had refused to take "no" for an answer.

This project was beginning to reveal a noticeable pattern of "will" far greater than my own, like wind blowing through the trees. I was curious to know what was floating in on that breeze. So I quickly assembled the materials and began to create her replacement panels. Although it began as a duty, before I knew what was happening I was immersed in a delightful process of discovery, with expressions and freedoms I had never felt before. By instinct or anticipation I must have known this might occur, because I had already made a crucial decision. I had selected wider doors and had reduced the height considerably so that the proportion would be more suitable for paintings with design, expression, and development. In bringing them to fruition I found depths of intuition, creative confidence, and instinctive beauty that would have been blocked in the past by my classical work habits and layers and layers of paint development. Moreover, it all happened very quickly. In less than two weeks I had her new paintings ready for delivery.

No sooner had she hung them on her wall than she called me again. "Glenda, could you paint one more panel for me? I sold another one." The wind through my trees was moving up to gale force! This was just the beginning of a phenomenon.

That was the beginning of a two-year project of painting angels on ash doors! In each case, within days of completion, someone arrived at my studio to behold and declare, "That's **my** angel!"

What never ceases to amaze me is the angel's perfect choice of ash doors for a medium. In addition to being a door, it provided a **doorway** for expanding my awareness, and a metaphorical expression of the angels' own place in the universe. After all, do they not stand as guardians of the doorway to higher awareness and life? One thing is certain, as a classically trained artist, I would never have selected such a medium without external intervention. Most certainly, I would not have accepted it as a catalyst for stylistic evolution. What a sense of humor, or irony, was moving my world.

That's getting ahead of the story, however. The cornerstone and pivotal reason behind the unfolding events was about to be revealed in February of 1994. My client's friends from the church (who had purchased the first two panels) contacted me to commission more angels and wanted a personal meeting. They came to our home where they saw "The Lamb and The Lion" for the first time. It was a warm and moving experience and the beginning of a deep and meaningful friendship for us all. On that day they commissioned me to paint seven archangels for their chapel.

That project consumed most of the approaching spring and gave us a chance to become better acquainted. This was a Christian organization that was more than simply a church. At the time of its founding in 1939, this non-denominational fellowship declared that it would remain open to all people and open to all aspects of Christian truth, hence its name "Christ Truth League." Since that time it has taught and served quietly on its beautiful fourteen acres in Fort Worth, Texas. In keeping with the ecumenical ideal, its outreach has largely been through publishing and through generous support of other Christian fellowships. Their chapel, which is a charming mix of traditional and modern motifs, is situated in the midst of an exquisitely landscaped garden. Altogether, this lovely environment has a serenity and spirit of sanctuary that can refresh the weariest soul. It certainly had that effect on me.

Dr. Applegate, the senior minister at that time, was deeply inspired by "The Lamb and The Lion," and asked me if I would display it in the chapel and provide a Sunday service. As it turned out, the day we chose was also the first day all of their new angel paintings would be in place on the walls.

When that day arrived, it was a dazzling spring morning without a cloud in the sky. I was happy about the good weather, although it did not seem to matter as far as the painting was concerned. Regardless of inclement weather preceding or following a presentation, at the time of our arrival, conditions would always clear and be fine. More than once, rain would be pouring through gusts of wind until the moment we needed to expose the painting to the elements. Then, a spontaneous clearing would occur! These were common and predictable miracles that I had come to take for granted. Nevertheless, I was glad that the birds were singing and the sun was shining that

Sunday. It was just one more thing I would not have to worry about ... or so I thought!

Just as the benediction was being said, the sky darkened and the elements clapped a loud Amen with thunder and lightning. In just moments, rain was pouring in sheets. In every other instance where weather had presented some obstacles, a little patience always provided safe passage. But it would not happen on that day, nor for three days. Day and night, it rained continuously. The only thing that was clear was the fact that the painting had to remain in the chapel.

For the first time in the life of the painting, it would be transferred to someone else's care. The painting was not insured outside of our custody (not that I had any real worries), therefore the church accepted its new responsibility with a bit of insecurity as well as reverence. To that end, the members and ministry slept overnight in the church and maintained a seventy-two hour vigil around the painting which proved to be as much for their benefit as for the painting. Many dreams and visions were brought to consciousness as well as soul-deep bonding with the love and natural grace of Jeshua's portrayal. The most important dream was brought to Debbie Truman, the church member who had purchased the first angels. She was told that "The Lamb and The Lion" was home.

Had this dream not been divinely inspired, that would have been an audacious presumption. That's because I had never mentioned to anyone other than my husband that we were looking for any other place to house it! Actually, it was several weeks before she worked up the courage to mention her dream, and even then, only when I first remarked that our visit to the church with the painting was the highlight of our spring. Her message caught me by surprise, as did the whole proposition. Having had no knowledge of Christ Truth League prior to February, I had once more been brought to face the unexpected. However, as I surveyed the possibility, it became obvious that housing in their chapel met every criterion I had wanted, including the fact that it was open seven days a week to all people for prayer and meditation. It was easy to find, reverent, quiet, and beautiful.

Arrangements were finalized, and by June "The Lamb and The Lion" and "The Flame of Love" were happily situated in their new home. It was a wonderful resting place for them after a long journey. Every part of the journey had been facilitated by miracles, but only then, as I beheld the two paintings hanging contentedly with their escort of archangels did I begin to realize how important were the patterns of synchronicity, which had moved through my life, bringing divine will into clear view. Synchronicity must surely be the dynamic process of miracles unfolding. If only we would listen and respond.

The paintings could now flourish in their own sacred ambiance. As for myself, I continued to paint angels on ash doors until early 1996. Perhaps that was the length of time needed for me to pass through **my** next doorway to greater understanding and personal unfolding. I sensed the presence of angels as forces of love moving into an environment or situation, a non-intrusive yet powerful presence that provided extra measures of grace, protection and positive opportunity. Every now and then I would catch a glimpse of some passing light out of the corner of my eye or an unusual fragrance that appeared out of context. Nevertheless, my perceptual field was still grounded in the common dimension we call "normal"-- whatever that means. For me, gaining an expanded awareness of love was far more important than any visionary manifestation that might accompany a celestial presence. I painted angels because a hunger in my soul had been aroused to know and to behold that form of higher life. Even more than that, the act of surrender which had been so painful in the beginning was now becoming a submission to joy as I allowed the forces of higher consciousness to pour through me and bring to fruition the beauty of its presence.

As life moved on, there was another significant change ... learning to proceed without "The Lamb and The Lion" as my constant companion and inspiration for both living and painting. At first it was like having good friends move away, yet still feeling the ghost of their presence in all the familiar places. Then I spilled into a reverie of treasured memories. As time passed by, I realized that nothing important had been lost. Jeshua was still with me in spirit, and the richness of my personal growth was more than my hopes had envisioned. I no longer needed a sitter in front of me, or a vision to behold. The "vision" now was the beseeching of my heart which desired nothing less than a chance to honor and serve a higher guidance, as well as the privilege of connecting with my fellow man, soul to soul. The threshold had been crossed, and a new world of contribution and creativity welcomed me.

I surrendered to inspirations from my daily meditations, prayers, and creative activities, where I found a vital and even greater connection with the Living Christ. There have been other visitations with full sensory perception with him through the years. However, I seek them less and he offers them less, not because he denies me anything I ask. But rather, because there is far greater comfort and enlightenment in a relationship based on faith that grows daily through the heart. There is greater dimension to this than anything I could have imagined in 1992.

Courage to speak the truth and share my stories would be the next chapter of my life. Through sharing the sacred, my sanctuary was being attained, not as a passive retreat, but as a dynamic, living process that would guide the rest of my life and work.

Chapter 8

The Heart's Greater Vision

Before the painting left for its new home, I devoted several days sitting with Gunnar on our living room sofa, just adoring the painting that had graced our home for more than two years. From the first day of its completion this had been its home, where it rested between days of travel. I sat in rapt attention hoping for some final message while memories of our life together washed over me.

Almost daily for the last two years visitors would drop in unannounced, sometimes from around the world. Each time I saw their heart leap I felt it all again as if for the first time. Countless miracles were reported, and the very joy of spreading the connection was a miracle in itself. The most touching moments were those of children, especially the babies who had emotional responses unexplainable by conditioning. I remember one amazing dialog between a mother and her three-year-old daughter, which she held up to eye level with the painting. They were inventorying the painting in a kind of 'show and tell' way.

The mother would ask, "Do you see the tree?"

"Yes," the girl would nod.

"Do you see the lion in clouds?"

"Yes, Momma."

This went on, item by item, until the mother finally asked, "Do you see the man?" The girl pursed her lips and shook her head in a firm, "No." What was this, her mother thought? And so, she asked again, and actually several times more. "Do you see the man?" Each time the answer was no. So, the mother changed her question, "Well, what **do** you see?"

Without words, the little girl looked up, with her arms outstretched to heaven. No words were necessary, and we all felt a sense of wonder at her response.

Once I was awakened by a telephone call at two AM from a man named Unimi who had just been imprisoned from a raid on his village in one of the troubled countries of Africa. His home and much of the village had been destroyed. His wife, who was eight months pregnant, was rounded up with others and carried off to who knows where. In very broken English, and a voice stricken with fear and grief, he told me his story and begged for help from anyone who could intercede on his behalf. I asked how he got my number and why he called me, of all people. The one thing he had taken to prison with him was a picture of "The Lamb and the Lion" that a missionary had left for his church. It had my number on it, and he knew I had a connection with One who could help. In addition to Divine guidance, I discovered that Dr. Applegate of Christ Truth League had been that missionary, and my call to him later in the morning brought the relief that was necessary. A few months later I received a letter from Unimi and a picture of him with his wife and a beautiful baby boy.

Marvelous and tangible transformations occurred in the lives of so many who saw the painting. Physical, mental, and emotional healing occurred before my eyes. But, most of all a change was happening in me. What I had known as "me" was beginning to lose its boundaries. Instead of defining my experience by what happened **to** me, I began to savor life as what happened **through** me.

This would grow, and in 1996 Jesus would appear again and request that I share with others what he had spoken to me. My agreement to do this was not without reservation, but it led eventually into the joy and privilege of addressing many audiences live with the lectures now recorded as *"Conversations With Jesus,"* and the two books, *"Love Without End, Jesus Speaks"* and *"The Keys of Jeshua."* And now, on this twenty-second anniversary of beginning that painting, "The Way to a Greater Life" is going to press.

I have been asked many times if there were other visitations. The answer is yes; there were several. They were, however, mostly of a private nature; and, they seemed to happen as a gradual transition from sensory perceptions **of our first meeting to inner awareness of a lasting connection through Spirit**. I came to recognize his voice as that of Higher Consciousness offering guidance for my life. Many times as I wrote the books, I could feel his personality in that Higher Consciousness, and it was as if we were sitting together at the writing desk. Perhaps we were, but it was no longer necessary that I have sensory confirmation, because a higher perception had taken over.

As a matter of fact, I think I would look back on the original visitations with some disbelief if it were not for the personal transformation it set in motion. Anything that is true also has a lasting effect on our life, and it matures as it propels us into growth. It shows in our life and work. It changes us, and indeed becomes a new paradigm for how we view life from that point forward. Would any of us expect a child to go through twelve years of school and still think and speak as a six year old?

The philosopher of religion, Hans Jonas, suggested that a natural sequence exists in each person's maturing from objectification to internalization. This is to say that our objective experience must be integrated into personal experience before it can become an evolutionary force in our lives. According to Jonas, this is not only true with personal transformation, but also for generational progressions. One generation's objective and conceptual orientation becomes the next generation's guide to inner transformation.

The next level of sequential development, when we apply ourselves to the utmost in personal growth, occurs within us as individuals when we actualize into our being the experiences, ideas, and inspirations that have formed our lives. Every great teacher recognizes the need to translate objective experience into subjective awareness from whence a meaningful communication emerges from self to others. Only through empathy, and other similar abilities from person to person, can we achieve transmissions at this level.

Essentially the experience we call mystical is the experience of our interconnectedness. Above all, the mystic vision is an 'experience of the heart', and as such, mysticism leads to compassion. The vision that transforms us at one moment becomes the cause of further change. Because we are the world (to put the matter simply) the vision that transforms us will also change the world. In our interconnectedness, the consciousness of each will reflect itself back into the consciousness of all. Human evolution arises out of the transformation of individuals.

Dr. Erich Newman, one of the foremost successors to Dr. Carl Jung, once proposed that the human being is essentially *homo mysticus,* which is to say that the ground of our being comes from an inexpressible reality of Higher Being. While the mystical experience is immediate, and by its very nature unitive, there exists within us the basis for growing toward greater realization of those moments, in addition to assimilating them and applying them to external reality. By this our relationship with the environment changes for the better, and we ascend to our own higher ground. He believed that the major phases of any person's life could be forecast and measured through observations of growth in consciousness, how it develops and in what direction. How far, and where, it will go is unique for each person.

However, he was not referring to intellectual development, disciplined intention, or any accumulation of spiritual teachings and practices. The mark of expanding consciousness is not the product of aspiration alone; nor is it the result of imagination, clairvoyance, or clairsentience. It is largely the result of opening the doors and windows of one's being to a greater light while maintaining personal integrity and coherence of Self within a greater flow, which has a life of its own. On a mighty river, we all float either in unity or disunity, through purposes that are known or yet to be revealed. Questions about our place and contribution in community are answered and confirmed only by transformative growth revealed in the progress of a person's life and the lives of those consequently benefited. Those who appear least among us, yet who have attained the most transformative growth are not the least among us, regardless of external appearance.

True purposes are shaped by unitive participation in a grand flow of life. We are always part of one or many flows of energy, consciousness, and social interaction. Within these grand migrations of spirit and manifestation, either we can find our own nobility, or we can become overwhelmed by our smallness against its grandeur. Those who have the lower perspective (and that would be most people) look for goals and purposes to strengthen ego identity on their raft within the river. Even through worthy goals, defensiveness, fear, and all manner of disability may limit their prospects for true success, not to mention their vision. I remember from my days as a university teacher, how much energy was wasted on campus politics, ensnaring great minds that otherwise would have accomplished wonderful things. When designed by the ego, life becomes competitive rather than fluid.

Throughout known existence, all forms of energy—from the spin of planets, to solar systems and splendid universes, to the lightness of consciousness and spirit—all travel through curving cycles of time and space.

What we now explain as deja vu and prophetic revelation may be understood better in the future as recycling consciousness that was unrecognized on its first or second pass through. All manner of possibilities for the future are with us now, but without enough concurrence of events or supporting realities to activate or even expose them. A classic example is the helicopter Leonardo Da Vinci designed in the sixteenth century. Nicola Tesla is another. Despite the suppression and termination of his research by vested interests still feeding an older cycle of consciousness, most of his ideas are still valid. When the next cycle of consciousness brings them around, with enough unification of coordinating science and reality, they simply will not be stopped. The final fruition of this technology may be as different from Tesla's designs as the modern whirly-bird is from Leonardo's sketches. However, there will be no doubt that an earlier vision has resurfaced. Often, this is the tragedy of men and women who see too far ahead of their time. Indeed we see this truly in the life of Jesus and many who chose to follow him. I look forward to a major return of that blessed state of consciousness in unison with all other realities that have progressed to support it. When that happens, what transformation we will experience on this earth!

Everything progresses in waves and cycles. Only light makes a straight line, and it too participates with curvature by refracting when forced to bend. Otherwise it will disperse into particle form to be openly distributed through the curvature of time and space. Perhaps we can thank gravitational fields for causing space-time curvature. Or perhaps gravitational fields have simply conformed to a greater generative force uniting all forms and possibilities into a curving space that enfolds and unfolds without end.

Because of space-time curvature, even literally of the earth, we can never see too far down the road. If you look out over a large flat field on a clear day, you can see for a few miles until the horizon presents a boundary. The earth has curved out of sight. If you climb a tower, its greater elevation will provide a longer angle of vision and you can see a few miles beyond the first horizon. From a helicopter or airplane, your angle of vision increases with every degree of altitude. Even from the moon, which removes all earth-bound horizons, there is the back side of the earth that can only be revealed as it spins on its axis.

There is no environment or circumstance unaffected by space-time curvature. What does this have to do with mystical vision and mastery? A lot, actually, and rarely understood. Most of the time, we are thrown off-course by curves we did not expect. It could be a curve in the road, a curve in our health, our partnerships, in the economy, or by any sudden loss. Ideally, we will be forewarned of approaching curves, and be able to make informed corrections from a greater angle of vision. But, unfortunately, that doesn't always happen.

The greatest masters of life have learned to find a greater angle of vision through elevations of consciousness. From that heightened perspective they can make better decisions, with more love and wisdom about how to ride with the flow and not to make sudden dangerous changes to stop or resist it. Like a skillful surfer, a master of consciousness studies the waves of life and knows when and how to ride them. He immerses himself in union with the flow and then becomes the wave.

We can find within our heart our own portion of quantum space, our infinity, where time and space lose their ability to bind us. The heart of our being allows us to see 'through' distractions and misdirection clamoring for our attention. From within the heart we can see vast distances that burn through curvatures of time and space that have baffled even our imagination. Through the heart we can live in simple solitude or find the right wave for more dynamic involvement with life.

Why have so many men and women, who are so capable and worthy of success, failed to achieve it? They were stopped by curves in their way, which they could not see beyond! In addition to natural curves, there is exploitation of change by those who would seek to profit by misleading others. It might interest you to know that the basic meaning of 'wicked' is twisted. It came from the twisting of string to make the wick of a candle. What an ironic connection to light.

What is the remedy? Jesus and all the great masters have given us one seminal word to guide all our actions. That is faith. True faith allows us to unite with beneficial prospects in life, even if they have not been fully revealed. It also stimulates our instinct to step outside a flow of events not serving our good and seek a higher perspective. If we observed that power in its true and highest meaning, faith would invoke powers of the heart capable of navigating through all twists and turns along the way. Unfortunately, its meaning has been watered down somewhat by platitudes and maudlin sentiments about faith to the point that some use it to justify apathy, lack of consciousness, or misdirected trust.

One might say that mystical union is an extraordinary moment of Faith that gives us the courage to release our defenses and become more than we ever thought we could be. It is an insurgence of spirit into our immediate, existential experience in such a manner as to cause a stronger presence of being and outflow of genuine and unconditional immersion into life.

The ordinary becomes miraculous and yet it does not cease to be ordinary. As the well-known Zen Buddhist saying has it: "Before enlightenment, trees are trees and mountains are mountains. After enlightenment, trees are still trees and mountains are still mountains." For convenience, we speak of progress or a path, but in actuality there is neither progress nor path. There is simply an ongoing and continual surrender of intellectual knowledge to greater heart-wisdom, if only subliminal. In the midst of daily life, those mysteries which animate the entire cosmos and which make all of us one family, become part of us.

Both the world of our self and the world that we once thought of as not-self are made new because we now see the underlying unity of existence. We know ourselves as part of a greater whole in which the smaller self no longer clamors for attention (or derails our happiness). The whole manner of our seeing and viewing the world has changed. The truth of things is the truth of their being. "Truth," as Annie Besant said, "is only truth when you have learned to live it."

This is why mystical ecstasy has such an overwhelming impact on us and seems so far removed from the ordinary world. Such heightened experience shatters in an instant the illusion that our subjective and objective worlds are separate, or even real. In a mystical state the barriers dissolve, new elements rule. The world of awareness and the world of matter fuse into one stupendous matrix of connection, penetrating and encompassing everything in a blaze of glory beyond description. In the presence of a greater light we cannot see our own. We lose our personal definition, our boundaries, as we live in the infinite splendor.

Our normal consciousness is an extremely dilute form of this splendor, like a droplet of water compared to an ocean of life. We are not able to perceive this almighty intelligence or its radiance because our sensory equipment is adapted to the environment in which we live. The veil before our eyes has been created by our senses, which respond only to a particular field of perception. Areas beyond that range are normally shut away from us. For instance, we cannot perceive electromagnetic waves with any of our natural senses. We can, however, see them through instruments and devices designed for that purpose.

Many energetic transmissions are beyond our sensory capability. For example, a moth can smell its mate from as far off as seven miles and a shark can scent blood two miles away. A bloodhound can detect the scent of a fugitive for scores of miles among thousands of other scents left by animals and human beings that walk over the same path. Bees find their way by polarized light imperceptible to human beings, and whales locate their prey with sonar-echo thousands of feet below the surface of the ocean. What worlds are hidden from us we cannot even imagine?

We may never know if Consciousness and Spirit are the same. Although, in considering the basic definition of consciousness we have a clue: "Consciousness" means **unified** mind. I can only think of three natural forces capable of converting mental activity into perfect unity. **The first and foremost would, indeed, be Spirit.** If so, that would make them similar in essence, with Spirit being the larger and greater force.

We also know there is an element in nature, which supports and nurtures all natural phenomena. It is this force which is credited with miraculous powers in all the mystical reports from the past. Prana is the Sanskrit word for "life force," which has been vividly invoked and described in Vedas. In Chinese culture it is referred to as Chi. Within Eastern religious or spiritual traditions Kundalini is described as an indwelling spiritual energy that, when awakened, can purify the subtle system and ultimately bestow a state of Divine union upon a seeker of truth. This can be compared to Holy Spirit in Christian traditions, although usually regarded more as Spirit than energy. On the other hand, we cannot totally dispense with Biblical reports that flames appeared on the shoulders of the Apostles at their awakening. Regardless of its name or our perceptions, it is felt by all, and has been universally held to be the provider of miracles, mystical visions, and exceptional gifts of understanding. It is sufficient that we call it Life Energy.

There is a third compelling factor that orders all things through attraction. We could say this is the heart (or many hearts) of existence. Through unseen magnetism, we respond to life in an orderly fashion because of the many points and fields of attraction. All forces and forms collaborate into unity around centers of attraction, or many such points expanding wider and wider in their sphere of influence. A 'single point' may be only hypothetical, or it may be precisely literal. It could be the beginning of a line, a direction, or hub of a pattern or a universe. It can be mathematically decoded or merely inferred.

From petals around daisies to galaxies where movement and cohesion fall into centripetal progressions, there is organization around a central confluence of energy. Every matrix is composed of countless points of attraction seeking unity in relation to larger, more powerful organizing systems. Without this organizing force no symmetry, no equilibrium, and no progressions of anything could be observed. Light itself converts from a wave to single points that disperse into infinite patterns of propagation.

Measurement, comparison, and even creation all begin at some particular point. It could be an inception of thought, fertilization of an ovum, or the first note of a musical composition. By daring to rise from the numbing similarity of a random field, a word is spoken, a single photon of light is emitted, and order begins. There is now a connection from which to draw the second, third, and fourth points into a design or system. Chaos can be resolved. As the field expands, not one but many organizational centers are necessary.

Single points with unique presence in a unified field cannot be overestimated for their value to a living universe. Multiplicity and variety of single points allows for the shifting of influence within a cohesive flow of energy. Without points of influence shifting into new configurations and possibilities, all of existence would be a frozen field without resolution or potential for growth.

As Living Souls we are each unique points within the Body of God. Every individual has extraordinary value just by being present and aware. Each is a sole repository of consciousness, experience, determination and love. Not only that, our multi-layered complexity allows us to serve on many planes of existence. We are born of the flesh, and yet we are conjoined as children of God. We share communities from small to large, and within each one we have our moments of influence. We are both mortal and immortal. We are each rare and irreplaceable, although most people have no clue about that truth and act accordingly. The irony is we confuse our uniqueness with discrimination by differences. Only through love can we rise to a full appreciation of our self and those with whom we share life.

This is immensely important to recognize lest we fail to see the importance of love to our fulfillment. By a seeming paradox we are asked to honor the uniqueness of our personal being, life, and experience, while surrendering our separation from God and from those with whom we share life. Some have come to believe that our greatest spiritual attainment comes only from losing our self completely to the whole. That opinion may hold some value for some people, for a while. But, it does not answer the riddle or resolve the paradox of mortality and immortality. The answer is that the self we created through experience, beliefs, goals, and relationships is no more than that. It is created by us, and unique only by the differences we assign to ourselves in comparison with others. Thus, our ego defenses are fragile, and sensitive to assault. The Self that was created by God is distinctive by origin, holding its own inimitable place in the order of existence. There is nothing to defend, alter, or fix.

The paradox of unity held together by countless spheres of individual awareness is the essence of a mystical riddle. To fully grasp it requires exactly what the great masters have taught us. Surrender all vestments of ego, immerse oneself into the ocean of unity, and yet maintain the purest and most radiant expression of individuality and self-worth. The Soul's light will shine through all the complexities of life. This is a formula for mysticism that can stand up to all the revelations and pressures of a scientifically driven age of technology and objectivity.

Let us also consider the possibility of there being some creative force greater than anything we can yet detect or measure as physical energy. It might be present in the atom and sub-nuclear particles without ever being identified by any means known to science. The Power of Creation which brings the universe into existence is both mind and matter. For David Bohm, all of matter is just frozen light. Incomprehensible to the intellect, this is the Source which becomes clearer and more perceptible in a mystical state. Most often we feel it as the unconditional supply of life or love. Unconditioned and limitless, this greater force is capable of creating any kind of world or substance that can be conceived, or even beyond conception. It is the Power behind the phenomena of life. It is the Power behind faith-healing and miracles, as also behind time, space or causality, even emptiness, and timelessness.

What amazing worlds, what incredible forms of life, and what unimaginable planes of existence are possible! The theory of relativity, the progressive discovery of sub-nuclear particles, black holes, pulsars, quasars, antimatter, and the expanding universe, all point to the conclusion that, with every advance in knowledge, the universe has not become simpler and easier to understand, but more complex and more difficult to grasp by the intellect. What undreamed of conclusions will scientific research lead us to next, even in the course of one century? No one can predict. How could we hope to explain the Divine merely with our intellect?

In a lecture given in London nearly eighty years ago, Dr Annie Besant spoke of a "wave of mysticism passing over the world." Such a wave seems to be apparent today. Many people are expressing their hunger, an inner yearning, for a genuine spiritual experience. Not satisfied with the answers which either science or religions offer, many have sought teachers and gurus of varying degrees of reliability. In many religious traditions, there has been a re-awakening to the esoteric wisdom hidden beneath the outer forms. By its very nature esoteric wisdom participates in the mystical. At the same time, scientists are pointing beyond its former materialistic boundaries to what we might call 'meta-science.' Is this a subtle admission that consciousness may be primary?

It is our human destiny to be fully conscious—not simply to theorize, to have opinions, to conjecture, to believe, **but to really know. To know** is to fully meet every experience, at every moment of time, in every place. Out of that encounter, **which is truly the mystic experience,** arises a new and natural way of living that is both simple and beautiful, a way that shows commitment to the cosmos, to our fellow human beings, to life itself, a commitment of the personal self, and to the One Self seated in the heart of all beings. Our actions and our presence in the world are of one accord, in harmony with the ethic of love, compassion, and truth.

Chapter 9

The Soul's Eternal Light

"Ye are the light of the world. A city that is set on a hill cannot be hid." (Mt 5:14)

The light of the Soul just IS, but it is very difficult to see our own light, because we are inside the experience of being it. We live in such a tightly connected network of light: spiritually, physically, and from others we often miss the glory of light revealed in us and to us. The fact is, we were born in the light. We discover this through living, asking many questions as we go.

How is it possible for us to create subjectively such a complete and amazing world, which fully coordinates with equally amazing worlds others have created for themselves? How is it that every part of our world, even our mistakes and silliness, are somehow substantiated by a much larger reality that responds to our every creation; even if at times it requires some correction or amendments? Have you ever wondered how you can envision or desire something from within your personal and subjective world and then receive it or have it supplied by someone you have never seen or dreamed of before?

The answer is that light provides a constant and common communication system for everything in this universe. It carries wishes, intentions, and prayers as if they were sent on a telephone line. It connects and transmits messages to all parts of existence ranging from energy waves and particles to the complex forms of suns and galaxies. This integrated medium of communication is composed of countless filaments or strands of light that move through and connect all dimensions of existence. The matrix of light is the constant that contains, unites, and adapts each of our personal creations into a larger range of possibilities.

Light affects us on every part of our being: physical, emotional, mental, and spiritual. It defines every level of the universe that we are capable of perceiving, and empowers and stabilizes many aspects of existence that we are not capable of perceiving. On the next page is a picture of an apple. It may not look like any apple you have ever seen, and no, it is not a microscopic picture of molecules in an apple. This is a holographic film which contains the exact electro-magnetic resonance of a whole perfect apple imprinted on a special kind of glass. When laser light is projected through this image, we have the image of an apple floating in space. (Picture 2)

This holographic phenomenon utilizes the same binary system of communication and encoding that underwrites all of creation. Everything has its own radiant energy signature, and every signature is a differentiated part of a vast energy field. An energetic signature includes everything from subatomic particles, to molecules and forms, along with all the components of consciousness. What facilitates its unity and also projects it into manifest reality is light.

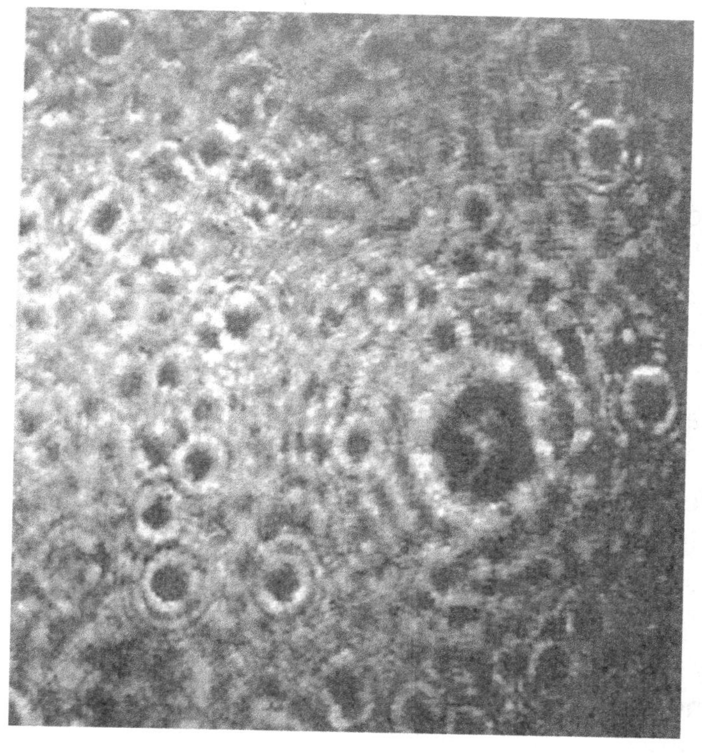

Just as a visible apple emerges when laser light passes through its energy imprint on holographic film, so too, when light passes through the radiant energy signature of our being, an image of who we really are emerges. It is usually greater than we expected.

Everything that has ever been, continues to exist in energetic memory and potential. Everything that was ever intended for creation is simply waiting to be activated. In fact, the latest reports of interstellar research are suggesting that the whole universe, including all that has not yet taken form, was created in less than two hundred thousand years. This is an instant in universal time.

In his messages to me, Jesus said that every part of creation still exists energetically; and, everything that is yet to be is already present as a latent pattern. If the universe is a giant bank of energetic records and potential, waiting to be awakened by light, what does that say about our ability to stir possibilities in our self we have hardly dreamed about? Creative forces of love, intention, and consciousness bring coherence to us through light, by which our greater potential is also made evident. This has powerful suggestions about our ability eventually to survive or transform a limited organic life form!

We are living Souls existing potentially far beyond the physical we now see! We have intrinsic ability and powers of communication far beyond our typically limited channels for connection and influence. You and I are pure energy-light in its most beautiful and intelligent configuration. If you could see yourself under a powerful electron microscope and conduct other experiments on yourself, you would see that you are made up of clusters of ever-changing particles in the form of electrons, neutrons, photons and so on. So is everything else around you. Energy is constantly changing beneath the surface and we control it all through our consciousness. From this perspective, the only difference between body and soul is the greater density of our physical form and the fact that it must one day release its component particles into a lucid flow for renewal and redemption.

In the Book of Genesis we are told that the first act of creation was light. In the Book of John we are told that in the beginning was The Word, meaning Logos or consciousness. Are light and logos the same? Everything I have discovered about the wholeness of life seems to indicate they are. We cannot encompass the entirety of God, but we can walk in the light of a Higher Consciousness.

Those who have achieved enlightenment call it that for good reason. It is not incidental that the most common response to some new or regained realization is, "I see." One of the great similarities of light and consciousness is that they both create **and** result from conditions of integration, order, and harmony. It is not yet known if light is the absolute constant for the whole of existence (or merely presumed to be), but it is the constant of our ability to measure, predict, or understand anything about this universe, which is why we cannot measure anything faster than the speed of light. That does not mean such a thing cannot exist or be postulated to exist. It means we cannot comprehend it at this time, because our consciousness and all the instruments of our consciousness are innately facilitated by light.

In many ways light is a paradox. It is both a particle and a wave. Its wave bundles flow in reliably straight lines, yet photons can appear suddenly and spontaneously across distances. It can be measured and yet it is the constant by which everything else in the physical universe is measured. It has predictable qualities, which are seemingly absolute, and yet it is completely relative to the condition in which it is observed. Unlike every other physical element, it seems to have no end to its life.

For our personal life, light provides an interface between our personal reality and the universe so that we may be conscious of our personal place within the whole. It further provides a connection between ourselves and the Divine.

While we give all credit to the Author of creation, light has been an instrument of **manifestation** we have been living in and with ever since. It also ignites and manifests our own creations.

This seems to be an eternal constant in Jesus' message to us, 1 John 1:5-7 "This then is the message which we have heard of him, and declare unto you, that God is light, and in him is no darkness at all. But if we walk in the light as he is in the light, we have fellowship with one another."

Quantum physicists tell us that an object does not exist independently of its observer! Simply the act of observing an object causes it to be where and how we observe it. If this is true, our observation, our attention to something, and our intention, literally creates that thing. This is scientific and proven.

Naturally, we cannot observe all things happening, but let's consider that the great field of consciousness has that ability. Now, let's make one further consideration: that the Great Observer is observing us. It's a staggering thought, but nothing, including ourselves, can exist independently of co-observation. Within that field of recognition and communication **we and the Observer become one through shared light.** As the Oneness between our Self and Consciousness is consummated, we can see the fullest and truest resolution of science and theology as the Oneness of our union.

But, wait a minute! If everything is light, why do we also experience darkness? What is that about? From dark and rainy winter nights to cycles of relative darkness and relative light in cycles of the seasons, we experience quite different levels of luminosity; although none of us have ever seen absolute darkness. The vacuum necessary to create such a thing would not permit the existence of life much less any observation of it.

Observation of these cycles is just another exercise of consciousness. Yet, we alone, have created our ***belief*** in darkness as if it were a force containing power. We have projected meaning into darkness as having "substance," and we become afraid of a mere shadow. We have allowed darkness to symbolize and give illusory body and meaning to our losses, emptiness, or separation, and along with that we have created a shadow side of our being. We have believed in this strongly enough to make it real.

That delusion has also fostered our belief in polarity, which requires the invention of darkness to oppose and question our certainty of the light. When we are being afflicted by doubts and uncertainty, our anxiety tries to assign dark motives to forces we do not yet understand. Often when we have only partial understanding or confidence about something, instead of realizing that we need more light on the subject, we look for opposing forces to assign the cause of our unknowing. Tragically, we fail to understand that by adding more darkness (through negative thoughts and actions) we only increase our sense of separation and polarity. There is no polarity "out there," except that we, or someone else, have created it by empowering the opposite ends of a limiting condition.

Naturally, as creatures of the light, we must have enough light to supply our comforts, needs, and understanding of life around us. As with any other deficiency, here are slight pathological symptoms when we have too little light. The correct response to that signal would be to ask, "What light is missing in this situation? How can I discover and supply that light?" Instead, we often ask, what forces of darkness are conspiring against us? The sad thing is that the force of darkness is only a delusion that will breed more delusion if reinforced. The only real solution is to remember that unity multiplies light.

It can help to look for a third person (or persons) to resolve the differences and provide an extra portion of light.

The third reason we believe in darkness is that it represents some unknown which has not yet been revealed. In this case, we simply need to stay with our certainty and strengthen our integrity about what is and is not so. There is an acronym for FEAR: False Evidence Appearing Real. Our tendency is to run from the darkness, because we have an instinctive sense for what is not real. A better solution is not to invent darkness from which we run, but to blazon with light the trails on which we walk.

In all of creation, light was the first manifestation of Being. Before there was light there was a void (nothing). In all references to it, both spiritually and physically, light is the constant of **all that is.** Light always refers to Being and never to nothing, or even to doing. Even when we flip a light switch, we are not causing the light. Are just releasing what is available and ready to shine.

Basic to all our beliefs in darkness is that we have not yet centered ourselves in the power of our own BEING. As Shakespeare put it, "To be or not to be, that is the question." As we are told more powerfully in The Keys of Jeshua, "I was to conquer death, not by miraculous powers or even by prayer, but by the body and blood of MY BEING. Except that I am one with you and you are one with me, we can do nothing for one another. The same is true for all mankind. Through our joining in love, which is compassion; and the unity of spirit, which is peace, light is brought to the world and all is accomplished."

The fourth reason we believe in darkness is that such beliefs contain the negative feelings we have about ourselves or others. Darkness represents the hidden areas of our heart and life, hidden either out of forgetfulness, denial, uncertainty, or unworthiness. We all have deeds or thoughts of which we are ashamed, and so we create a place in which to hide them. The covering for these deeds or thoughts is our belief in the reality of darkness. From an enlightened perspective, this seems very silly, but we do it anyway. It's like a kitten that hides in a paper bag, thinking because she can't see out, she also can't be seen.

In Romans 6:23 we are told "The wages of sin is death." If physical death is a simple dissolution of material form into a larger and lighter essence, and God is love, the only death that ever could bind us would be our own declining ability "to be." Such a condition would come about without judgment, simply as a result of cause and effect. If there is any judgment at all, it would be by our own heart and mind. We are our own worst judges, and we execute our judgment by ceasing to be a Soul worthy of holding its light in the universe. If all "being" is light, then because of unseemly thoughts and deeds, our increasing inability "to be" would create a shadow existence capable of annihilating the Soul's radiance. Without some reconciliation to the light, a soul could feel very lost as its light fades to an ember under the shadows of its own dark covering.

An interesting observation I have made about troubled souls is that they cling to others in the darkness and yet starve for love because darkness has no substance for nourishment or to be shared. Even though we can hide together in darkness, we cannot put a spoon into the bowl of darkness and offer it as a food to others. It does not exist. We cannot light another's candle with darkness, for there is no power in delusion. Although many may cluster in darkness, there is great aloneness. There is a pivotal point at which we discover the impotence of darkness, and it loses its hold over us. This is the moment at which the light of our being assumes the steering wheel and takes us into the river of love. We return to our pursuit of unity.

This is why Jesus instructed us to forgive without ceasing. Include yourself in that. Your life and the life of others depend upon it. Anyone who has sinned, has also once known the light, and can know it again. By assigning power to sin, more darkness is created, and more light is lost. By casting power on the greater potential for light, sin is released.

We will not and cannot bring to light that which we are not willing to BE. Whatever we have done or thought, which we cannot also BE, will linger in the shadows. This is because light **is Being,** and **Being is light**! When Jesus said to take our light out from under the basket, he meant to stop defining our lives by negative actions that we hide, and ego pretenses that we show. Instead, we must BE our life! BE the answers we would like to find, and the changes we would like to see in the world.

Whatever you can BE with all your heart is good. In your Being is the light. In your non-being is darkness.

Whatever you can embrace, expose, and affirm will come into light.

And last, but not least, we often believe in darkness because we are afraid of the truth that light will expose. We are afraid we are not up to the responsibility of what will be revealed. Nevertheless, there comes a point when we make a **decision** that walking into the light IS OUR LIFE. At that moment everything changes. This is the moment when we assume responsibility not only for our actions but for our contribution to others. We have been alone in the shadows, and we hunger for sharing the light.

Then, spontaneously a connection occurs, which every ordinary sense would have claimed "impossible." That connection may bring elements of another world, or possibilities in this one we thought were out of reach. Perhaps they were beyond our grasp only moments before, but not out of sight to a higher consciousness. Through love, consciousness, or the constant of light, it was instantaneously moved into our world without delay or resistance. We have all witnessed the power of prayer or the power of heart-centered desire. Somehow, miraculously everything moved around in our world and made the impossible possible. If it were not for the presence of God within us, there would be no force capable of reaching to realms we cannot see and moving the desires of our hearts to us.

Like the holographic film, our lives are waiting for the light of consciousness to pour through and create a new vision of what can be, or perhaps what has always been. In turn, **we become the light** that passes through the film of others' lives. What we see may often be surprising but also comforting in its deeper truth.

This is the heart of mysticism, and its consummation is enlightenment. In the end we must ask one final question: If God's first creation was light; if we, in the image of God, are a light into the world; if all of creation is sustained and revealed through light, then what is there left to be lighted?

All that would be left is our interconnection with one another, our world, and the universe. The only two commandments Jesus gave to us precisely speak to those needs: To love God with all our heart, mind, and Soul, and to love others as our self. The only real unknown, the only variable, and the only real challenge is what can come of our connection with God, with others, and experiences of the earth. What may come of our responsible, loving, and united state of being?

To contemplate this, to live this, and to expect its fulfillment in every fiber of our being is to be a light in the world. That state of being cannot be accomplished by toil, competition, logic, or permission from ordinary reality. The light of our Soul transforms to a sun as we climb to the high places of consciousness and dare to honor what we see. In such moments the light of our Soul conveys the light of heaven to the earth.

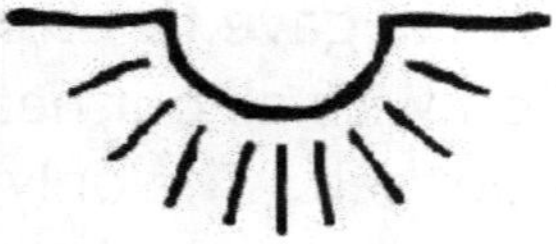

Chapter 10

Apparitions of Christ

For two thousand years, faithful believers have reported visions of their beloved Redeemer. Sometimes they were sensed as a soft whisper in the ear, a gentle touch on the shoulder, perhaps a blinding light, or a full blown physical appearance. Are these visions the result of wishful thinking, or is more going on than meets the normal eye?

Whatever such events represent, we must admit their frequent occurrences throughout history, to both the faithful and the unfaithful. Indeed, one of the pillars of belief in the early church's formation was the apparitions of Christ.

The first apparition was reported three days after Jesus' crucifixion. This event, in fact, was the defining moment of a new religion. Easter morning is dawning on the Sea of Galilee. The first rays of light travel like a guided laser over the water and the hillsides, as though searching for a particular point in eternity to illuminate. Inside a dark cave only a rumble of shifting rock can be heard. Suddenly this rumble reveals itself to be a stone rolling away from the closure of a tomb. Just one spark of light finds its way through the slight jar in the passage. But it is enough to gently caress a reclining body that can barely be seen in the darkness. Suddenly, as if to ignite nuclear fission, the sunlight, and the "Light of Life" explode into a blinding radiance. This is a light that has no direction and casts no shadows. The "explosion" rolls the stone closure completely away, light pours out of the tomb even brighter than the sunlight, and Jesus emerges. His body has a growing translucent quality giving evidence of its transformation into some higher substance.

We can imagine him wrapped in his stained shroud, walking, almost gliding on air, to the garden shed of the cemetery to look for any garments that might have been left behind by a gardener. He is about to leave the cemetery when he sees Mary Magdalene approaching the tomb. Sunrise after the Sabbath would have been the first moment anyone could have attended his body. She is shocked to see the stone rolled away and the body missing. She mistakes Jesus for the gardener, and asks "Who has taken my Lord?" Then she is even more startled to realize that it is Jesus wearing the gardener's attire. She wants to embrace him, but hesitates. Her caution is confirmed by his words: "You cannot touch me," but please, carry the good news to others that I am alive." She departs with great joy.

Later that day he appears from "nowhere" to join two men walking on the road to Emmaus. He walks with them and visits with them through dinner, when they finally recognize who he is. Then he suddenly vanishes into "nowhere."

Within days, Jesus appears to the other Apostles and gives evidence that his material solidity has returned by eating food and allowing Thomas to touch his wounds. After teaching them the miracle of resurrection and many other wonderful things, which even the scriptures say were never written, he transforms his body into heavenly matter and ascends into the clouds. But what is heaven for those who witness, is infinite potential for him. He continues to visit all the faithful for the next 40 years until the end of the generation to which he was born. The Book of Acts has numerous accounts of such appearances. One was to Ananias, and the most dramatic was as a blinding light to Saul on the road to Damascus. This is when Jesus called Saul (who became Paul) from his persecution of the Jews. Later Jesus came again to warn Paul in Corinth, and once more in Jerusalem it is written that Jesus "stood by him" to sustain his faith. In an apocryphal account it is written that Jesus appeared at the moment of his mother's death and escorted her to heaven

The first generation of those who knew Jesus seemed to have no problem with paranormal appearances of him after his resurrection. Indeed, these mystical moments of reunion stirred inspiration, often leading to great acts of faith. Such experiences and beliefs permeated early Christian mystical literature, although this subject would become a challenge for later theologians to reconcile. The first to take on this subject was St. Augustine. In his *"Literal Meaning of Genesis"* he discusses three types of visions: corporeal, imaginative, and intellectual. A corporeal vision is when all of the normal senses recognize a physical presence of Christ. These occurrences were frequent enough they could not be dismissed. St. Augustine defined imaginative and intellectual visions as being subjective, even though the cause may have been Divine.

Mystical appearances of Jesus, whether seen by the eyes or simply felt in the heart are pivotal to the Christian faith. Ironically, they have been among the most controversial and often suppressed experiences as well. Non-believers are simply skeptical, and many believers have difficulty reconciling such "living events" with controlled doctrine that does not allow for spontaneous elevations of consciousness, especially when it happens to a lowly congregation member, or an urchin, rather than a Priest or Bishop.

Human debates notwithstanding, Jesus' presence as a Spiritual Being has continued to descend upon whomever it chooses - from beggars to Popes - throughout the ages. These events transcend all doctrine and exceed all limitations in the dauntless and vigilant pursuit of Spirit to reveal a more sublime relationship with the Infinite than we could ever imagine, much less control.

Extraordinary events have the power to direct our attention beyond limited reality, and cause us to seek for more of the exceptional. In the accounts of St. Anthony, who suffered greatly in the desert from evil spirits, we read that upon his victory over the torture "Our Lord appeared visible and joyous." Then Anthony asked, "Where were you when I needed you?" The Lord answered, "I was here just as I am now, but I wanted the pleasure of seeing how staunch you are." This story offers a poignant answer to many who might ask, if such appearances are real, why does he not appear and cut short events of suffering or even disaster?

Perhaps these extraordinary encounters with a Higher Presence were never intended to solve our problems or to intercept the patterns of life that we must master for ourselves. More likely, we are being offered extraordinary evidence of a boundless universe in which our problems take on a new perspective. This most certainly resulted from Jesus' appearances to Saint Francis, Saint Germaine, and Archbishop Cyprian who all entered a higher level of service through transcendental perception.

Records tell of Jesus' appearance through the centuries to many others, including St. Gregory the Great, St. Theresa of Avila, and St. Ignatius Loyola, and well into modern times with such visionaries as John Wesley, Joseph Smith, Charles G. Finney, and General William Booth. Many times he came in a blinding light; sometimes through acts of healing; and often in the faces of those to whom charity had been shown. In some cases, these visitations were bestowed as a confirmation of faith, but not always, as with Saul, who had no faith at the time he was greeted by the light of Christ. Often visions of him came as compassion offerings, unconditionally given to clueless recipients.

One of my favorite stories was published in The Church of Scotland Magazine about a "Comrade in White," who appeared frequently on the battlefields of Argonne in World War I. Another remarkable story was told by the Senior Surgeon and Physician at Swansea Hospital, who had witnessed the healing of a thirty-five year old woman, totally crippled and tied to a bed. After a visitation with

Jesus she led a normal life, with very little assistance. No medical facts can explain what happened. Stories like these go on and on, as if to remind us that what we think is so is only a reflection of our deepest fear holding us to the shackles of limiting belief.

Rich or poor, literate or illiterate, healthy or harmed, troubled or happy, believers or non-believers, there seems to be no respect of person as to who will receive a vision ... and, no reason, except to remind the recipient that he or she has been touched beyond the limits of structure and worldly conditioning. This relentless pursuit of freedom, unity, and love is what I have found to be most characteristic in all dimensions of Jesus' life.

Will there ever be a scientific explanation of such phenomenon? Probably not, although there may be meaningful scientific analogies, once it is understood that faith is inseparable from science, especially in the new frontiers of quantum reality. Mysteries are all around us, and the greatest, most fascinating mysteries of life are to be savored and not resolved. Perhaps the most amazing and humbling discovery of modern science is the fact that ninety-nine per cent of all existence is not only invisible to our senses and instruments, but also without mass or configuration. Even the one per cent that comprises our physical universe is solid only because of relatively stable configurations of energy. Among the greatest scientists - including Niels Bohr, Max Planck, and Werner Heisenberg - it has been conceded that there is room in a rational universe for incomprehensible wonders. Albert Einstein said: "The most beautiful emotion we can experience is the mystical. It is the power of true art and science. He to whom this emotion is a stranger, who can no longer wonder and stand rapt in awe, is as good as dead. To know that what is impenetrable to us really exists, manifesting itself as the highest wisdom and the most radiant beauty, which our dull faculties can comprehend only in their most primitive forms - this knowledge, this feeling, is at the center of true religiousness."

Our perceptions are focused most of the time upon the one per cent of existence that can be seen, heard, and touched. And, then we are surprised when some evidence emerges from the remaining ninety-nine per cent. I think it is natural to be cautious about things we cannot see, feel, or control, yet if we carried that caution to its ultimate degree we would have no place for faith and no outreach for God. Whenever we relax or release the filter called "self" and lose ourselves in play, service, conversation, sharing, imagination, meditation, prayer, study, or sleep we shift our focus from survival pursuits into larger patterns of connection with unlimited possibility. Most often our connection with the infinite is not a mystical revelation, but a quiet and personal epiphany at moments when we realize that the miraculous and the mundane are one and the same. At such moments we see clearly that everything is already before our eyes awaiting only a shift of perception. Marcel Proust said that, "The real act of discovery consists not in finding new lands but in seeing with new eyes."

There is no question that the exploration of human consciousness is the last great frontier. Well in advance of our scientific progress, two thousand years ago the life and teachings of Jesus stimulated an expansion of consciousness that will see no end. In many ways he ignited this through demonstrations of what seemed like paranormal mastery of life. Yet the power behind his miracles and the reason for them was his assurance that they were *not* paranormal for him. They were NORMAL for a level of faith capable of embracing them. Indeed, he promised that at some point, "All these things and more YOU shall also do."

His miracles would have had no lasting value if they had been performed merely to impress others with powers beyond the grasp of humanity. There was no vanity in him. The value of his life was not in what set him apart from, or above, humanity; rather, in what united him with it. By that same standard, if apparitions are regarded as something weird and freakish, the sanctity is lost. I believe there is something within each of us that yearns for a higher reality and opens to it with uncontrived wonder.

There are many ways through which God appears to all of us. It could be through inspiration, an unexpected blessing, a new friend, inner guidance, wise counsel, or the Holy Scriptures, to name only a few possibilities. Any appearance of God is an extraordinary apparition, which we usually take for granted. So close is God to us that we mistake the Holy Presence for the air we breathe. Is there any wonder that, at times, a gateway to enlarged perception is necessary to get our attention? It is not that any one of us is more exceptional than others, or singled out to carry a higher light. It's just that some are present when such a gate is opened, or perhaps were used as instruments to open a gate for others. At times the immortal spirit of Christ walks through that gate and we see him.

Life is more fluid than our perceptions normally suggest. Space adapts to the requirements of a given purpose, and time is simply a loom that weaves the threads of destiny, causing the events of our life to approach and disappear. Daily I was seeing evidence of the promise he made long ago that, "I am with you always."

Perhaps there is another factor in our humanness, which calls apparitions to us. Beyond our mortal frame, in dimensions that are not governed by time and space, we must surely be conscious of our place in the quantum universe. It could be no other way, considering that even the least of particles has within it a quantum potential. When Jesus talked about the Kingdom of Heaven he compared it to the size of a mustard seed. I seriously doubt that he was diminishing its size, but rather he was revealing that even within the tiniest creations is the pattern of something immense and grand. This is what I mean by the quantum nature within each of us. Perhaps in our hunger to know and see more, to step outside the ordinary, we occasionally release our mortal defenses, if only for a moment, and receive the blessings of a greater life.

Chapter 11

An Endless Journey...

Today many reports of mystical vision are available for study and comparison. Apart from the traditional mystics, whose frame of mind was essentially religious, who underwent various spiritual disciplines to attain a mystical state, there are also poets, philosophers, scientists and scholars who had a sudden visionary experience, once or several times in their life, without the practice of any orthodox religious or esoteric discipline. Pascal, Bucke, Tennyson, Wordsworth and Tagore were living examples of this type of mystical vision. According to his own statement, a few moments before his epileptic seizures, Dostoevsky experienced a state of lucidity and bliss to which he attributes a lifetime of more than ordinary experience.

How are we to account for this phenomenon? From immemorial times the mystical state has been held to be a vision of Divinity, God, Allah, or Brahman, or any other name for the Creator. Libraries are filled with books penned by the mystics themselves, or of theologians and other scholars supporting their views. Such lives have been characterized by religious devotion, involving seclusion from the world, renunciation, submission to Divine Will, contentment, austerity, even penance with extreme love of God. Their models of devotion have been considered prerequisite for success in the mystical quest. This point of view is probably too restrictive, however. It does not allow for how mystical ecstasy has also been bestowed upon others in the course of normal life in the midst of worldly pursuits. Nor does it explain such phenomena occurring with children. There have been well-known mystics in whom spiritual bliss began in childhood and became a natural state of experience. There is no rational explanation for these extraordinary cases of mystical consciousness.

There are still many scientists who, like Freud, treat the whole phenomenon of religion as an illusion, a pathological condition due to the repression of more natural instincts. If this were true, the whole irrational fabric of faith should have been completely dismissed long ago. But, strange to say, the reverse has happened. Mystical vision and the miracles associated with it have assumed an urgency and importance that far exceed the previous two centuries. This shows how erroneous the intellect can be. The widespread thirst for self-awareness or the intrinsic side of nature is utterly inexplicable in the light of modern psychology and science.

It is incredible that the learned world should still be in the dark about a phenomenon that has been at the base of civilization and culture, through which all the moral and intellectual progress of mankind has been made. Our religious impulse and the lure of spiritual ecstasy has been part of human life as far back as history extends. We have irrefutable evidence of how the human mind has been occupied with a higher force of consciousness almost from the beginning. Facilitators of such experience appear on the scene from the remotest periods. All of the vanished civilizations, about which we have any knowledge, were completely dominated by religion. The current world religions, some of which date back as much as 4,000 years, have held onto the imagination of their believers as tenaciously as those preceding them in timeless history. In this sphere of the human mind, science is but a helpless spectator.

The world has never been so tense, so on edge. We live under an overhanging threat of holocaust because we are violating an almighty law of our nature. We hardly have awareness of this law. **That is, humanity is the steward of consciousness. By comparison to that duty, all other responsibilities and accomplishments pale!**

It is not by mere accident, delusion, or the plotting of charlatans and priests that the major religions of the world came into existence. Had that been the case, such coherence of movement and such influence over the hearts and minds of people could not have lasted for so many centuries. The tragedy is that the custodians of faith attached more importance to formulism than to the basic teachings of the religious founders. They missed the higher way of consciousness and fell into rigid structures that could not withstand the pressures of social evolution.

It is not by coincidence that the great spiritual luminaries were born to reveal in their being a mode of life and pattern of behavior, which for the multitudes would teach the laws of harmony and assist with evolutionary processes at work. In fact, it is the impact of their teachings and the order they established which prepared the soil for the great achievements even of modern science.

The parents, grandparents and great-grandparents of the pioneers of science were, in most cases, deeply religious men and women with faith in God and a righteous way of life. At the same time, many of the great thinkers and scientists failed to understand the importance of religion as the outward symbol of the most deeply rooted evolutionary impulse in human beings. They failed to note that all the revealed scriptures of mankind had a common purpose, which is to implant an ideal of infinite possibility and to prescribe the way of life and the mode of behavior necessary to achieve union with it through our own potential. **In other words, the aim was to present an evolutionary ideal and the methods to achieve it.**

Religion came to prepare the ground for an evolved state of consciousness capable of supporting true science. The advent of science did not come by random discovery and opportunity. It marks another stage in the evolution of human consciousness. Moreover, it is changing with every turn of the earth. Science of a hundred years ago hardly resembles science of today. We do not see the immensity of this evolutionary power because of an erroneous impression that evolution is only a force of external adaptation, whether physically or socially. Most scientists of the human mind still believe consciousness is local and limited to the brain, and that it has remained relatively unchanged for the last twenty thousand years. From their view the brain is believed to gather and store data necessary for survival, manage bodily functions, and to solve problems as they arise in the environment. But, only in special cases does it anticipate or supersede a problem.

To the contrary, our consciousness has charted every course of our history, and has done so with creative means yet to be fully described much less explained. A fascinating feature of human consciousness is that it can never paint a correct picture even a few decades ahead of what will come. Or perhaps that is one of the great values of art and other intuitive pursuits—that future attunements can be seen around many bends in the road. I was always amused when someone would dismiss their lack of talent for painting by saying "I can't draw a straight line." I would always answer, "It's not the straight one that matter."

As discussed in chapter 8, there is a space-time curvature to all things. However, by envisioning what is possible, responding by instinct to opportunities that arise, and riding the great waves of life moving us forward, we will learn what we must know at the appropriate concurrence of events. The great intellects alive in the late nineteenth century could never imagine the state of information available to intellects alive today. In the same way we cannot enter the mind of those living a hundred years from now. There are extremely few who can think ahead of their time. Yet we are here, and "here" seems to be the only place we would understand! Tomorrow we will be exactly where we need to be also, even though we cannot see far beyond our current horizon.

In summary of these observations, there are three suppositions we may safely claim about consciousness until such time as we more fully understand it.

1. Human consciousness gains strength and vitality through forces of circumstance that push it to expand, adapt, and solve new predicaments.

2. Essential to our survival is an ability to climb to some tower of observation where life beyond our current paradigm may be ascertained by way of exploration, preparation, imagination, parable, prophesy, ecstasy, or attainments of character necessary for achievement.

3. In all past civilizations when this ability to gain elevated perception and knowledge was overwhelmed by the ruthless momentum of political or material forces, collapse was inevitable and all was lost.

The aim of this great survival force is to coordinate evolution within the body collective whereby we attain to consciousness exceeding our current realizations. If the evolution of consciousness does not keep pace with the speed of material progress, oppression and stagnation will ensue. History stands witness to the inflexibleness of fossilized structure. What happened to many ancient civilizations, even after their rise to lofty heights, and often with staggering technological achievements, is that they ceased to keep pace with the demands of life to move forward. Dominance is a terrible price to pay when it cost one's place in the forward flow of existence.

Decay from within, not marauding enemies, disease, or famine leveled the once victorious and ascendant nations. When consciousness ceased to evolve, the time-defying pyramids and the awe inspiring temples of Egypt could not save their populations from falling helplessly into decline. Once-great civilizations, whose achievements are scattered all over the earth, have already paid for their ignorance of this one great mandate: **that spiritual evolution is the real goal of human life.**

There is a place beyond good and evil, a flow greater than all circumstance where we unconditionally embrace the best that life has to offer and reach for the stars. I love the ironic and mystically haunting passage written by Friedrich Nietzsche, a major 19th century philosopher. "Whatever is done out of Love always occurs beyond Good and Evil." There is no greater power of destiny than the grand flow of love. It exceeds all of our self-righteous proclamations of good and evil.

The real purpose for which science took birth is to explore our relationship to the universe and accelerate the betterment of humankind. From this point of view, science is not the end but the means to a greater end. Space rockets, skyscrapers and all the wonders of modern science, combined, will not be able to save our race, if we fall into ignorance of a higher drive within us all. Today, however, we have a new and unique challenge and that is to rise above the glamour and greed of externalized information and data—to not fall into confusion of this data base as a counterfeit of true knowledge. If Christ can be held to be the personification of complete and fulfilled Consciousness, then the anti-Christ is truly with us as the counterfeit of consciousness (in the form of distracting data—much of it being false), which fills every cubit of our modern life.

To find that special place within, where the boundaries drop between inner and outer awareness is the mystical work of each human life. In this place there is knowledge beyond what is supplied by common information. This is knowledge that sees what is possible by accessing what has always been so. The great mystics, in every culture and every belief form, held that vision for us.

One of my favorite emissaries of twentieth century mysticism is Thomas Stearns Eliot. I love the brilliance of his mind and the genius of his pen. But, more than that, he was a voice of secular enlightenment at a time when existentialists were bathing in the rivers of modern contempt for spirituality. He explored and measured the terrain of our inner landscape and taught the modern mind how to move with metaphysical grace even if the external world seemed to be a wasteland. He saw a miraculous infinity that still held wonder for the human heart as surely as it did for the minds of extraordinary scientists in his generation. Beyond war, he sought peace. Beyond apathy and material gluttony, he saw the mandate for spiritual replenishment. He gave the twentieth century a vision that is still hauntingly relevant for the new millennium. Many times I have read his work as a contemporary anchor for me in the flood of timeless visions I have received from Jesus. In fact, I used a number of Eliot's quotes in my first edition of "*Love Without End.*" Hopefully in this book I have conveyed more understanding about why that elasticity of perspective was necessary for my own centering of consciousness. One of my favorite Eliot passages, in which I find so much eternal truth, talks about our ultimate exploration. I think it is also one of the most powerful summations of how we are likely to experience mysticism in our modern moments of "now."

We shall not cease from exploration.

And the end of all our exploring
Will be to arrive where we started
And know the place for the first time.
Through the unknown, remembered gate
When the last of earth left to discover
Is that which was the beginning;
At the source of the longest river
The voice of the hidden waterfall
And the children in the apple-tree
Not known, because not looked for
But heard, half-heard, in the stillness
Between two waves of the sea.
Quick now, here, now, always--
A condition of complete simplicity
(Costing not less than everything)
And all shall be well and
All manner of thing shall be well

When the tongues of flame are in-folded
Into the crowned knot of fire
And the fire and the rose are one.

T.S. Eliot, from "Little Gidding"

Who's Who in the History of Western Mysticism

This document was prepared by Professor Bruce B. Janz of the University of Central Florida for the free use of scholars and students of mysticism. He has graciously consented to our use of it in this publication.

This collection only covers Western mysticism to about 1700, and does not imply any value judgment about mysticism in other cultures, or revelations that happened after 1700. This summary was originally constructed for one of Dr. Janz's university courses called "Philosophy of Western Mysticism," and it reflects the research focus for that original context. Hopefully, in future printings of our own book we will be able to greatly expand on his list.

The people and movements on this list are arranged chronologically, rather than alphabetically. It is by no means complete in reflecting mystical figures or texts in the West -- there are literally hundreds of them. Dr. Janz included writers and texts that seemed to reflect the high points of mystical writing. They do not represent a single tradition of mysticism. This list is intended only to mention the major figures. A good source should be consulted for more extensive biographies and discussions.

The biography given for each of these is very brief and intended only to identify the person. If "influences" are mentioned, they are only to try to identify major precursors to a particular person's mystical thought.

Pre-Christian Mystics and influences on mysticism

Pythagoras (c.580/570-c.500 B.C.E.): A Pre-Socratic philosopher. Founder of a major school of philosophy and religion that emphasized the mystical interconnections in numbers, nature, and the human soul. The natural and the ethical world were inseparable.

Parmenides (c.515-c.450 B.C.E.): *On Nature*, extant in fragments. (another of the Pre-Socratic's.) This extends Pythagoras by insisting that all that exists is unchanging and unified. Therefore, if something is changing, it is illusory. This paves the way for the two-world view important for much mysticism. *Influences:* Pythagoras.

Plato (428-348 B.C.E.): Sophist, Republic, Parmenides, many others. Most important of ancient philosophers. His philosophical system provides the basis of most later mystical forms. *Influences:* Pythagoras, Parmenides.

Aristotle (384-322 B.C.E.): Metaphysics, De Anima, Nicomachean Ethics. While Aristotle himself is not really considered to be a mystic, he is an important influence on later mystics, especially when combined with Plato by Plotinus, and also when Christianized in the high Middle Ages.

Philo (c.20 B.C.E.-c.41 C.E.): *The Contemplative Life.* An Alexandrian Jew who drew from Platonist tradition, Stoicism, and neo-Pythagoreanism to create a fusion of the active or virtuous life and the contemplative life.

Plotinus (c.205-270 C.E.): Enneads. The non-Christian, neo-Platonic basis for much Christian, Jewish, and Islamic mysticism. *Influences:* Plato, Aristotle.

Porphyry (c.232-304 C.E.): *Isagoge.* Compiled Plotinus' *Enneads*, and wrote a life of Plotinus. He was strongly anti-Christian, yet he became important in the history of Christian mysticism.

Proclus or *Proclusthe Lycian* (412-485 C.E.): *The Elements of Theology*. Athenian Neo-Platonist, who influenced Pseudo-Dionysius, and beyond him most of the mystical tradition. While respecting Plotinus, Proclus also amended his philosophical structure.

Christian Mystics and Movements

(1) Early Church

Ignatius of Antioch (c. 35-c.107): Christocentric mystic. For him Christ's death and resurrection take on mystical significance.

St. Polycarp (c.69-c.155): Had a mystical vision which foretold his martyrdom by fire.

Justin Martyr (c.105-c.165): First Apology. Used Greek philosophy as the stepping-stone to Christian theology. The mystical conclusions that some Greeks arrived at, pointed to Christ. *Influences*: Pythagoras, Plato, Plotinus, Aristotle, Stoicism.

Irenaeus (c.125-c.202): *Revolution and Overthrow of False Knowledge* (or Against Heresies). Irenaeus' work was directed against Gnosticism. He emphasized John's gospel, particularly the Logos, which became the voice of God that revealed itself to all people.

Tertullian (c.155-c.222): To Martyrs, Apology, Against the Valentinians, Against Marcion, On the Soul. Emphasized a faith that was a contradiction to reason. "I believe because it is absurd." First to use trinitarian (three-in-one) formulation for God.

Origen (c.185-254): On Principles, Against Celsus. Studied under Clement of Alexandria, and probably also Ammonius Saccus (Plotinus' teacher). He Christianized and theologized neo-Platonism. Each soul has individually fallen (emanation), and must find its way back to God (return) through the help of the Logos, Christ. Origen looks quite Gnostic at times.

St. Antony (c.251-356): *The Letters of St. Antony the Great*. Early hermit or solitary monk, and a model for later monasticism, particularly of his eremetical type.

St. Athanasius (c.296-373): Against the Gentiles, Apology Against the Arians. Bishop of Alexandria (328-73), wrote a Life of Antony, and was an influence on later Eastern Orthodox mysticism.

Gregory of Nazianzus (329-389): *Forty-five Sermons*. One of the Cappadocians, early church fathers.

Basil the Great (c.330-379): *Longer Rules*, Liturgy of St. Basil. One of the Cappadocians, early church fathers. He gave a mystical orientation to the monastic movement. Gregory of Nyssa (c.335-c.398): *Dialogue with his Sister Macrina concerning the Resurrection*. Believed that the universe existed as a harmonious order emanating from God. One of the Cappadocians.

Augustine (354-430): De Trinitate, Confessions. Important source for much mediaeval mysticism. Brings Platonism and Christianity together. He emphasizes the soul's search for God, made possible by the illumination of the mind of God. *Influences:* Plato, Plotinus.

(2) Mediaeval (Catholic and Orthodox) Church

Pseudo-Dionysius the Areopagite (writing c.500): The Celestial Hierarchy, the Mystical Theology, and The Divine Names. Originates the distinction between kataphatic and apophatic theology. *Influences:* Plotinus.

John Scotus Eriugena (c.810-c.877): Periphyseon. Eriugena translated Pseudo-Dionysius from Greek into Latin. He holds that humans are a microcosm of the universe. That which is shared, the essence of all things, is God. *Influences:* Plotinus, Augustine, Pseudo-Dionysius.

Bernard of Clairvaux (1091-1153): *Sermons, De diligendo Deo,* On the Love of God. Cistercian mystic. Promoted a mystical vision of rhapsodic love, in which the Church is described in erotic terms as the bride of Christ. His love-mysticism had the tendency to be anti-intellectual, as in his disputes with Abelard.

William of St.-Thierry (c.1085-1148): *Golden Letter, On the Contemplation of God, On the Nature and Dignity of Love.* A Cistercian contemporary of Bernard's, William also emphasized love-mysticism, but with subtle differences from Bernard in his use of Augustine.

Hildegard of Bingen (1098-1179): Scivias, *The Book of Divine Works, Letters.* Early German speculative mystic, reminiscent of Isaiah or Ezekiel at times. She was greatly respected in her time, both for her writings as well as for her music and art. *Influences:* Augustine, Bernard of Clairvaux.

Victorines: Hugh of St. Victor (c.1096-c.1142), Richard of St. Victor (d. 1173): On Sacraments. Hugh is the more important of the two. He argues for a close tie between reason and mysticism.

Francis of Assisi (John Bernardone) (1182-1226): *Canticle of the Sun.* Founder of the Franciscan order, which emphasized self-renunciation and poverty. Francis approaches nature mysticism at times, particularly when he sees God in all living things.

Albertus Magnus (1206-1280): The teacher of Thomas Aquinas. In the tradition of Pythagoras, emphasized the essential unity of science and mysticism. *Influences:* Augustine, Pseudo-Dionysius.

Beatrice of Nazareth (1200-1268): The Seven modes of Sacred Love. Belgian Cistercian mystic. Associated with the Beguines. *Influences:* Augustine.

Mechthild of Magdeburg (1207-1282): The Flowing Light of the Godhead. Strongly feminine images in mysticism. Devotional mystic. Associated with the Beguines. *Influences:* Bernard of Clairvaux, Hildegard, Gregory the Great.

Bonaventure (John Fidanza) (1217-1274): *The Mind's Road to God, The Tree of Life, The Life of St. Francis.* Franciscan monk, and the architect of the philosophical, theological, and mystical side of Francis' thought. Mysticism in the

Augustinian tradition. *Influences:* Augustine, St. Francis of Assisi, Victorines.

St. Thomas Aquinas (1224-1275): Summa Theologica, *De Anima*, many others. Dominican monk and the greatest Catholic theologian and philosopher. Late in life, he had a mystical experience which caused him to question his scholastic past. *Influences:* Aristotle, Augustine, Pseudo-Dionysius, Eriugena.

Ramon Llull (c.1235-1315): *Great Art, The Book of the Lover and the Beloved.* Franciscan. Legend has it that Llull wrote 200 works, was an alchemist and a magician. He also worked on the logic of science. The "Great Art" is the scientific and mystical calculation of the interrelations of all things. *Influences:* Bonaventure.

Angela of Foligno (c.1248-1309): *The Book of Divine Consolations of the Blessed Angela of Foligno*. Mysticism is based on the facts of Christ's life and death. *Influences:* Francis of Assisi, Bonaventure.

Marguerite Porete (d. 1310): The Mirror of Simple Souls.

Meister Eckhart (1260-1327/8): *Sermons, Parisian Questions* and *Prologues*. [Some English-language selections from his writings are available.] Dominican monk. One of the most important early German speculative mystics. Eckhart is the first of the so-called "Rhineland" mystics. The Sermons were in German, the academic works in Latin. *Influences:* Pseudo-Dionysius.

Hadewijch (Adelwip) of Brabant/Antwerp (13th century): Letters, *Poems in Stanzas, Visions, Poems in Couplets.* Belgian Beguine. One of the greatest exponents of love mysticism. *Influences:* Plato, Plotinus, Pseudo-Dionysius, Gregory of Nyssa, Richard of St. Victor.

Jan van Ruysbroeck (1293-1381): The Adornment of the Spiritual Marriage (Spiritual Espousals), *The Sparkling Stone, The Book of Supreme Truth.* Flemish mystic, sometimes considered one of the Rhineland mystics. Outlines the stages of the mystical life. *Influences:* Eckhart, Hadewijch.

Henry Suso (1295-1366): *The Little Book of Truth*, The Little Book of Wisdom (Horologium Sapientiae). A Rhineland mystic. *Influences:* Eckhart.

Gregory Palamas (1296-1359): Eastern Orthodox mystic. *Influences:* Pseudo-Dionysius, Athanasius.

Johannes Tauler (1300-1361): *Sermons.* Rhineland mystic and Dominican. Tauler emphasized the inner person rather than outer works, and because of this became popular in Protestant circles in the Reformation, and later Pietism and Romanticism. He was part of the same community that produced the *Theologia Germanica*. *Influences:* Eckhart, Mechthild of Magdeburg.

Anonymous (c.1350-1400): Theologia Germanica or *Theologia Deutsch*. Important influence in the German mystical tradition. Luther rediscovered and popularized it. *Influences:* Augustine, Eckhart, Tauler.

Richard Rolle (1300-1349): The Fire of Love. Part of the "English school" of late mediaeval mysticism. Emphasizes the "physicality" of the mystical experience (feeling heat, seeing colours, etc.).

Birgitta (Brigida) Suecica of Sweden (1302-1373): Ascetic mystic. Heavily involved in political activity. *Influences:* St. Francis of Assisi.

Anonymous (c.1349-c.1395): The Cloud of Unknowing, [as modernized, see also early text] *The Book of Privy Council*. Part of the "English school" of late mediaeval mysticism. The emphasis on "unknowing" God is part of Pseudo-Dionysius' apophatic theology. *Influences:* Pseudo-Dionysius.

Walter Hilton (d. 1395): The Scale (Ladder) of Perfection, Epistle to a Devout Man. An Augustinian monk, Hilton was an English mystic.

Julian of Norwich (1342-1413?): *Showings* or Revelations of Divine Love. Julian was part of the "English school" of late mediaeval mysticism. Mystical experience that came at the point of death. The experience came with healing, and she devoted her life to understanding her vision. *Influences:* Pseudo-Dionysius, Aquinas (?).

Margery Kempe (c.1413): Mainly known as the biographer of Julian of Norwich.

Catherine of Siena (1347-1380): Il Dialogo. Italian. Mystic; advisor to Pope Gregory XI. *Influences:* Augustine.

Thomas à Kempis (c.1380-1471): The Imitation of Christ. Augustinian monk. Finest expression of *devotio moderna*, modern spirituality, which downplays the Rhineland mystics' concern with contemplation and speculative theology, and stresses the practice of simple piety and asceticism. *Influences:* Eckhart.

Nicolaus of Cusa (Cusanus, Nikolaus Krebs) (1401-1464): *The Vision of God* (1453), De Docta Ignorantia. German mystic. Part of the revival of Platonism in the Renaissance.

Cusanus was a speculative mystic who emphasized the incomprehensibility and paradoxicality of God. *Influences:* Plotinus, Pseudo-Dionysius, Eckhart.

St. Catherine of Genoa (1447-1510): Life and Doctrines, Treatise on Purgatory. Mysticism spurred in part by the abuse and neglect by her husband. Her trauma becomes mystical as she argues that purgatory is a stage on the mystical path, the final purification of the effects of self-love.

Teresa of Avila (1515-1582): Life, by Herself; The Way of Perfection; The Interior Castle. Spanish Carmelite nun. Formed the Discalced (Barefoot) Carmelites, with St. John of the Cross. Is very important for describing the stages of the mystical journey. *Influences*: Augustine.

St. John of the Cross (Juan de Yepes) (1542-1591): Dark Night of the Soul and Ascent of Mt. Carmel. Spanish mystic. (Discalced Carmelite) Both John and Teresa emphasize mysticism as union with God, attainable only in the denial of the self. *Influences*: Teresa of Avila.

Giordano Bruno (1548-1600): Hermetic philosopher, one of the most important philosophers of the Renaissance. Bruno advocated a kind of nature mysticism which had a strong scientific component to it.

St. Francois de Sales (1567-1622): The Introduction to the Devout Life (Philothea), Treatise on the Love of God. French mystic. *Devout Life* is a classic of French spirituality.

Louis Claude de Saint Martin (1743-1803): Theosophic Correspondence. While technically Catholic, St. Martin's mysticism follows much closer in the tradition of Boehme and other nature mystics. *Influences:* Boehme, Swedenborg, Weigel, Law.

(3) Non-Catholic Christian Mystics (16th-18th century)

Martin Luther (1483-1546): While Luther had a well-known antipathy to mystics, it is also true that there is the foundation of mystical life in his theology of the heart, particularly in his early thought. *Influences:* Augustine, Theologica Germanica.

Heinrich Cornelius Agrippa von Nettesheim (1486-1535): De Occulta Philosophia (1533). It is not clear whether to call Agrippa Catholic or not. He did not embrace the Reformation, yet many of his themes are much closer to Weigel and Boehme than to any Catholic mystic. His was a speculative mysticism, as much interested in magic and alchemy as in spiritual life.

Paracelsus (Phillipus Aureolus Theophrastus Bombastus von Hohenheim) (1493-1541): Another speculative mystic more interested in medical alchemy, astronomy, and natural philosophy.

Valentin Weigel (1533-1588): *Know Thyself* (1572). Weigel begins in the tradition of Rhineland mysticism, and moves to the speculative nature mysticism of Paracelsus. *Influences:* Eckhart, Tauler, Theologica Germanica, Paracelsus.

Jacob Boehme (1575-1624): Aurora (1612) [in German], Mysterium Pansophicum (1620), Signature Rerum (1622), Mysterium Magnum (1623). Lusatian Lutheran. A major figure in German mysticism. *Influences:* Eckhart, the Jewish Kabbalah, Valentin Weigel, Renaissance alchemy, Paracelsus.

Christian Knorr von Rosenroth (1636-1689): Kabbala Denudata: The Kabbalah Uncovered. A Christian Kabbalist. *Influenced* by the Kabbalah, Jacob Boehme.

Angelus Silesius (Johannes Scheffler 1624-1677): *The Cherubic Wanderer* [Hungarian version] (1657-on). Mysticism in epigrammatic couplets.

George Fox (1624-1691): Founder of the Quakers. *Influences:* Boehme.

Gottfried Wilhelm Leibnitz (1646-1716): Monadology. Usually thought of as a rationalist philosopher rather than a mystic. However, while it may be too much to call him a mystic, it is certainly possible to see the affinities between his thought and that of Cusanus, Weigel, Boehme, and other nature mystics. His most important contribution is to blend inner life with rationality; most Pietists (and most scientists) assumed them to be mutually exclusive.

William Law (1686-1761): The Spirit of Love (1752-1754). English mystic. Law is most famous for his devotional works (like A Serious Call to a Devout and Holy Life), but later in his life he became interested in Jacob Boehme, and wrote several mystical treatises.

Emanuel Swedenborg (1688-1772): Many works, including Arcana Coelestia, Heaven and Hell, The Heavenly City, *Divine Love and Wisdom*, etc. Swedenborg worked out a detailed understanding of nature mysticism, applying it to everything from the animal world to the spiritual world. He is one of the few mystics to have an active following to the present.

Friedrich Christoph Oetinger (1702-1782): Nature mystic, Pietist. *Influences:* Boehme, Weigel, Swedenborg.

Johann Gottfried Herder (1744-1803): Another person who is often not counted as a mystic, but who followed Leibnitz in attempting to blend science and mysticism into a kind of vitalism. *Influences:* Cusanus, Boehme, Leibnitz.

NOTE: After the 18th century, the influence of mysticism explodes in the **Romanticism** of Germany, England, and America. True mystics, however, remain few.

Jewish Mysticism

Kabbalah

Abraham ben Samuel Abulafia (1240-1291): One of the founders of the Spanish Kabbalah.

Moses ben Shem Tob de Leon (1250-1305): *Zohar* (The Book of Splendor). The most important writer of the most important Kabbalist document.

Moses Cordovero (1522-1570): *Pardes Rimmonim*, *Elimah Rabbati*, Palmtree of Deborah. Spanish Kabbalist. Cordovero laid the groundwork for the Kabbalist ethical literature that proliferated in the 16th-18th centuries.

Isaac Luria (1534-1572): Founder of the Lurianic Kabbalah, which is the modern version. Most modern Kabbalists follow Luria's version.

Hasidism

Israel ben Eliezer, **Ba'al Shem Tov** (Besht) (1700-1760): Founder of the Hasidim, the sect appearing during the final stages of the Kabbalah's development.

Rabbi Nachman of Breslov in the Ukraine (1772-1810): Martin Buber, the author of I and Thou (*Ich und Du*), calls him the last Jewish mystic.

Islamic Mysticism

Sufism has sources in sacred texts, the remembrance of Allah, and respect for those who exemplify the straight path of Islam through and beyond explicit injunctions of the law.

Hasan of Basra (d. 728): Early advocate of ascetic piety. Hasan emphasized the Koran or Qur'an as the standard of right and wrong, which in turn emphasized the fear of God.

al Hallaj (d. 922): The Ta wa-sin Tried and executed for claiming that God had come to dwell in him.

al Farabi (ca. 873-950): Important philosopher as well as a mystic. *Influences:* Plotinus.

al Ghazali (d. 1111): First-rate Aristotelean philosopher, who extended Aristotle's theory of perception to argue for a kind of mystical perception that goes beyond reason. *Influences*: Aristotle.

Addendum: Terms, Trends, and Movements worth knowing about.

Alchemy: Alchemy, as often as not, assumes a Hermetic world view. Most people know alchemy as the search for the principle of transmutation of baser metals into higher (e.g., lead into gold). It is really broader, and represents the attempt to understand the connections in the world. Paracelsus practiced a medical alchemy, in which the body was a collection of balancing principles, and illness meant that the balance was off. If you take away the spiritual assumptions behind the alchemical forces, you have something remarkably close to Newtonian physics.

Beghards: male counterparts to the Beguines. Fewer, and less of an issue for the church at the time.

Beguines: group of female contemplatives, some of whom were mystics. They were condemned as heretics because they represented a challenge to the church's authority. Many important female mystics were associated with the Beguines, although the group was not necessarily mystical (some thought that mystical visions got in the way of practical life).

Gnosticism: Derived from Greek *gnosis*, knowledge. The Gnostic is one who claims esoteric knowledge about God and the metaphysical structure of the universe. There is a strong distinction between spirit and matter, God and the world. This position sometimes resulted in asceticism (the spirit must be liberated from the bonds of the flesh), and sometimes antinomianism (the material world is inconsequential, so there is no point in resisting carnal impulses). Some later mysticism (e.g. quietism) has the world-denying aspects of gnosticism.

Hermeticism: Followers of the legendary figure Hermes Trismegistus, or thrice-great Hermes, reputed to be an Egyptian writer. Much nature mysticism of the Renaissance found hermetic thought useful, because both understood the world to be intrinsically interconnected, and only understandable once those connections were understood. Hermes mixed with Pseudo-Dionysius was common fare in

Renaissance Italy, until Isaac Casaubon showed that Hermes was not who he said he was.

Kabbalah: Jewish mysticism that has its roots earlier than Christianity, but which flourishes in the Middle Ages and Renaissance. The Kabbalah struggles with the problem of how the human person can relate to a God who is totally other, and how that God relates to creation.

Monasticism: Although the tendency to live apart for spiritual devotion has a long history, it is closely tied to mysticism in the Middle Ages. The disciplines associated with mysticism have their most rigorous application there. The most famous orders are the Franciscans (St. Francis of Assisi, Bonaventure), the Dominicans (Thomas Aquinas, Meister Eckhart), the Carmelites (Teresa of Avila, St. John of the Cross), the Benedictines (St. Benedict), and the Jesuits (St. Ignatius of Loyola). The orders exist to this day, and continue to be places that encourage mysticism and contemplation (Thomas Merton was a Trappist monk, for instance).

Rhineland Mysticism: The Rhineland mystics were German mystics that follow the influence of Meister Eckhart. They tend to emphasize the search for the inner ground of the soul.

Sufism: The mystical bent in Islam is supported by passages from the Koran (or Qur'an) and is represented by the Sufis. Because there is a dominant emphasis on prophetic activism and legalism in Islam, Muslim tradition may be misunderstood as entirely inhospitable to mysticism. But the Sufi way, mainly transmitted through "lay orders" that trace their origin to some influential spiritual teacher, preserve a distinctively Islamic mysticism. Among these Sufi subtraditions are the Naqshbandi and the Nimatullahi, but there are several others. A few modern organizations (such as the International Sufi Movement led by Hidayat Inayat Khan) claim descent from traditional Sufis but do not require their followers to be Muslims. And recently the great Sufi poet Jalaluddin Rumi has been rediscovered as a source of inspiration by poets Robert Bly and Coleman Barks. However, most practicing Sufis affirm that they are Muslims.

Important Secondary Sources

The secondary sources in mysticism are quite varied. Sometimes whole works are devoted to the subject; sometimes chapters of quite unexpected works will be on mysticism. More general reflections on mysticism can be found as introductions or appendices to works on particular mystics or chapters in philosophies or psychologies of religion. And, many works on mysticism that seem to be reflections on the nature of mysticism turn out to be anthologies of writings of various mystics. Adding to the complexity, is the fact that the word "mysticism" has been used for all sorts of experiences, philosophical positions, personality types, writings, that is yet to be fully defined.

Glenda Green, M.A., D.D.

Glenda Green is one of the world's leading teachers of contemporary spirituality. Her teachings revolve around universal truths that are uplifting and enlightening to all people of all beliefs. From poetry to science, her teaching moves the reader to deep waters of understanding.

Within her body of work are some of the most complete, extensive treatments of pure science ever found in spiritual literature. World-renowned scientists have conferred with Glenda about these astounding revelations.

She has authored the best-selling books, *Love Without End...Jesus Speaks, The Keys of Jeshua,* the best-selling lecture series, *Conversations With Jesus,* and the internationally acclaimed portraits of Christ, *"The Lamb and The Lion," and "Jeshua."*

In addition to her writing and teaching, she is also acknowledged by the nation's leading scholars, critics, and museum officials as one of the world's foremost realist painters and spiritual artists. Her paintings are housed in major public art collections, including the Smithsonian Institution.

She has taught on the faculties of Tulane University and the University of Oklahoma. She is an exceptional public speaker in high demand. Her warm, witty and confident manner evokes our inner certainty of a higher awareness. With a clean energetic style, and masterful comprehension of the most critical spiritual issues, she offers her readers and listeners an exceptional opportunity to acquire a truer, more complete understanding of the universe and their own place in it.

Biographical references include, *North American Women Artists of the Twentieth Century: A Biographical Dictionary*, edited by Jules Heller and Nancy G. Heller; *Angels A to Z,* by James R. Lewis and Evelyn Oliver, 1996. *Who's Who in American Art,* (15th and 16th Editions); *Who's Who in the South and Southwest*, (17th, 18th, and 19th Editions); *Who's Who of American Women* (12th, 13th, and 14th Editions); *Dictionary of International Biography*, Vol. 16;

Also from Spiritis

Books by Glenda Green:

Love Without End: Jesus Speaks
The Keys of Jeshua
Anointed With Oil

Audio:

Conversations with JesuS (14 CD album)

Each CD is a full 90 minutes of powerful information from the original conversations between Jeshua and Glenda Green. This was her original public release. Experience the impact of Divinity in direct communion with a thoughtful and well-educated woman of our generation. Even though *"Love Without End: Jesus Speaks"* is a close transcription of these tapes, the recorded lectures provide an invaluable expression of human warmth, candor, and vulnerability that cannot be conveyed through the written word. They communicate to the heart with authenticity and immediacy.

Prayers and Meditations from The Keys of Jeshua (2 CD album)

This is an audio recording of 12 prayers and meditations from "The Keys of Jeshua" in Glenda's voice. It begins with an insightful introduction to meditation and prayer, and is enriched throughout with deeply heart-centered music.

Spiritis Publishing 1-888-453-6324
www.lovewithoutend.com

CPSIA information can be obtained
at www.ICGtesting.com
Printed in the USA
FSHW010459220120
66355FS